SIMPLE COOKING

WOK & STIR FRY

select editions,
vancouver

First published in Canada in 2001
by Select Editions
8036 Enterprise Street
Burnaby, BC V5A 1V7
Tel: (604) 415-2444 Fax: (604) 415-3444
email: main@select-books.com

This is a Starfire book
First published in 2001

02 04 05 03

3 5 7 9 10 8 6 4 2

Starfire is part of
The Foundry Creative Media Company Limited
Crabtree Hall, Crabtree Lane, Fulham, London, SW6 6TY

ISBN: 1-894722-20-5

Printed in Korea

ACKNOWLEDGMENTS

Authors: Catherine Atkinson, Juliet Barker, Gina Steer,
Carol Tennant, Liz Martin, Mari Mererid Williams and Elizabeth Wolf-Cohen
Editorial Consultant: Gina Steer
Project Editor: Karen Fitzpatrick
Photography: Colin Bowling, Paul Forrester and Stephen Brayne
Home Economists and Stylists: Jacqueline Bellefontaine,
Mandy Phipps, Vicki Smallwood and Penny Stephens
Design Team: Helen Courtney, Jennifer Bishop, Lucy Bradbury and Chris Herbert

All props supplied by Barbara Stewart at Surfaces

NOTE
Recipes using uncooked eggs should be avoided by infants,
the elderly, pregnant women, and anyone suffering from an illness.

Special thanks to everyone involved in this book, particularly
Karen Fitzpatrick and Gina Steer.

CONTENTS

SOUPS & STARTERS

FISH & SHELLFISH

MEAT

POULTRY

RICE & NOODLES

ENTERTAINING

HYGIENE IN THE KITCHEN

It is well worth remembering that many foods can carry some form of bacteria. In most cases, the worst it will lead to is a bout of food poisoning or gastroenteritis, although for certain groups this can be more serious—the risk can be reduced or eliminated by good food hygiene and proper cooking.

Do not buy food that is past its sell by date and do not consume any food that is past its use by date. When buying food, use the eyes and nose. If the food looks tired, limp or a bad color or it has a rank, acrid or simply bad smell, do not buy or eat it under any circumstances.

Do take special care when preparing raw meat and fish. A separate chopping board should be used for each; wash the knife, board, and the hands thoroughly before handling or preparing any other food.

Regularly clean and defrost the refrigerator or freezer—it is worth checking the packaging to see exactly how long each product is safe to freeze.

Avoid handling food if suffering from an upset stomach as bacteria can be passed through food preparation.

Dish cloths and dish towels must be washed and changed regularly. Ideally use disposable cloths, which should be replaced on a daily basis. More durable cloths should be left to soak in bleach, then washed in the washing machine on a boil wash.

Keep the hands, cooking utensils, and food preparation surfaces clean and do not allow pets to climb onto any work surfaces.

BUYING

Avoid bulk buying where possible, especially fresh produce such as meat, poultry, fish, fruit, and vegetables unless buying for the freezer. Fresh foods lose their nutritional value rapidly so buying a little at a time minimizes loss of nutrients. It also eliminates a packed refrigerator, which reduces the effectiveness of the refrigeration process.

When buying prepackaged goods such as cans or pots of cream and yogurts, check that the packaging is intact and not damaged or pierced at all. Cans should not be dented, pierced

or rusty. Check the sell by dates even for cans and packages of dry ingredients such as flour and rice. Store fresh foods in the refrigerator as soon as possible—not in the car or the office.

When buying frozen foods, ensure that they are not heavily iced on the outside and the contents feel completely frozen. Ensure that the frozen foods have been stored in the cabinet at the correct storage level and the temperature is below -0.4° F (-18° C). Pack in cool bags to transport home and freeze as soon as possible after purchase.

PREPARATION

Make sure that all work surfaces and utensils are clean and dry. Hygiene should be given priority at all times.

Separate chopping boards should be used for raw and cooked meats, fish, and vegetables. Currently, a variety of good quality plastic boards come in various designs and colors. This makes differentiating easier and the plastic has the added hygienic advantage of being washable at high temperatures in the dishwasher. (NB: If using the board for fish, first wash in cold water, then in hot to prevent odor!) Also, remember that knives and utensils should always be thoroughly cleaned after use.

When cooking, be particularly careful to keep cooked and raw food separate to avoid any contamination. It is worth washing all fruits and vegetables regardless of whether they are going to be eaten raw or lightly cooked. This rule should apply even to prewashed herbs and salads.

Do not reheat food more than once. If using a microwave, always check that the food is piping hot all the way through. (In theory, the food should reach 158° F (70° C) and needs to be cooked at that temperature for at least three minutes to ensure that all bacteria are killed.)

All poultry must be thoroughly thawed before using, including chicken and game hen. Remove the food to be thawed from the freezer and place in a shallow dish to contain the juices. Leave the food in the refrigerator until it is completely thawed. A 3 lb. (1.4 kg) whole chicken will take about 26–30 hours to thaw. To speed up the process immerse the chicken in cold water. However, make sure that the water is changed regularly. When the joints can move freely and no ice crystals remain in the cavity, the bird is completely thawed.

Once thawed, remove the wrapper and pat the chicken dry. Place the chicken in a shallow dish, cover lightly and store as close to the bottom of the refrigerator as possible. The chicken should be cooked as soon as possible.

Some foods can be cooked from frozen including many prepackaged foods such as soups, sauces, stews, and breads. Where applicable follow the manufacturers' instructions.

Vegetables and fruits can also be cooked from frozen but meats and fish should be thawed first. The only time food can be refrozen is when the food has been thoroughly thawed, then cooked. Once the food has cooled, then it can be frozen again. On such occasions the food can only be stored for one month.

All poultry and game (except for duck) must be cooked thoroughly. When cooked, the juices will run clear from the thickest part of the bird—the best area to try is usually the thigh. Other meats, like ground meat and pork should be cooked right the way through. Fish should turn opaque, be firm in texture and break easily into large flakes.

When cooking leftovers, make sure they are reheated until piping hot and that any sauce or soup reaches boiling point first.

STORING
REFRIGERATING AND FREEZING

Meat, poultry, fish, seafood, and dairy products should all be refrigerated. The temperature of the refrigerator should be between 34–41° F (1–5° C) while the freezer should not rise above -0.4° F (-18° C).

To ensure the optimum refrigerator and freezer temperature, avoid leaving the door open for a long time. Try not to overstock the refrigerator as this reduces the airflow inside and affects the effectiveness in cooling the food within.

When refrigerating cooked food, allow it to cool down quickly and completely before refrigerating. Hot food will raise the temperature of the refrigerator and possibly affect or spoil other food stored in it.

Food within the refrigerator and freezer should always be covered. Raw and cooked food should be stored in separate parts of the refrigerator. Cooked food should be kept on the top shelves of the refrigerator, while raw meat, poultry, and fish should be placed on bottom shelves to avoid drips and cross-contamination. It is recommended that eggs should be refrigerated in order to maintain their freshness and shelf life.

Take care that frozen foods are not stored in the freezer for too long. Blanched vegetables can be stored for one month; beef, lamb, poultry, and pork for six months and unblanched vegetables and fruits in syrup for a year. Oily fish and sausages should be stored for three months. Dairy products can last four to six months while cakes and pastries should be kept in the freezer for three to six months.

HIGH-RISK FOODS

Certain foods may carry risks to people who are considered vulnerable such as the elderly, the ill, pregnant women, babies, young infants, and those suffering from a reccuring illness.

It is advisable to avoid those foods listed below which belong to a higher risk category.

There is a slight chance that some eggs carry the bacteria salmonella. Cook the eggs until both the yolk and the white are firm to eliminate this risk. Pay particular attention to dishes and products incorporating lightly cooked or raw eggs, which should be eliminated from the diet. Sauces including Hollandaise, mayonnaise, mousses, soufflé, and meringues all use raw or lightly cooked eggs, as do custard-based dishes, ice creams, and sorbets. These are all considered high-risk foods to the vulnerable groups mentioned above.

Certain meats and poultry also carry the potential risk of salmonella and so should be cooked thoroughly until the juices run clear and there is no pinkness left. Unpasteurized products such as milk, cheese (especially cream cheese), pâté, and meat (both raw and cooked) all have the potential risk of listeria and should be avoided.

When buying seafood, buy from a reputable source, which has a high turnover to ensure freshness. Fish should have bright clear eyes, shiny skin, and bright pink or red gills. The fish should feel stiff to the touch, with a slight smell of sea air and iodine. The flesh of fish steaks and fillets should be translucent with no signs of discoloration. Molluscs such as scallops, clams, and mussels are sold fresh and are still alive. Avoid any that are open or do not close when tapped lightly. In the same way, univalves such as cockles or winkles should withdraw back into their shells when prodded lightly. When choosing cephalopods such as squid and octopus they should have a firm flesh and pleasant sea smell.

As with all fish, whether it is shellfish or seafish, care is required when freezing it. It is imperative to check whether the fish has been frozen before. If it has been frozen, then it should not be frozen again under any circumstances.

INGREDIENTS

As the recipes in this book demonstrate, wok cooking is not confined to Chinese and Thai ingredients. It is, however, with this type of cooking that the wok is most closely associated. The most fundamental ingredients, which give these cuisines their distinctive flavors, are listed below.

BAMBOO SHOOTS

These are the young, edible shoots of some kinds of bamboo and are widely available canned. Pale yellow with a crunchy texture, they come peeled—either whole or thickly sliced. Rinse before use and transfer any unused shoots to an airtight container and cover with fresh water. Refrigerate, changing the water daily, for up to a week.

BLACK BEANS

These small black, soy beans, also known as salted black beans, have been fermented with salt to preserve them. They have a distinctive, salty flavor and savory aroma. Often used as a seasoning in conjunction with garlic and scallions or ginger (as in black bean sauce), they are available either dried in bags or canned in brine.

To use either type, rinse well before using and chop a little, if preferred. The dried beans keep indefinitely, as will the canned beans, if kept in their liquid in an airtight container in the refrigerator.

CHILIES

Chilies are a common ingredient in both Chinese and Thai cooking and are available in many forms. Fresh chilies are easy to find and most supermarkets usually stock a range of various types. Add chili sparingly to food until you are familiar with each type. Your heat tolerance will gradually increase the more chili you eat.

To prepare fresh chilies, remove the stems and then halve them lengthwise. Remove the seeds and chop or slice the flesh as required. The seeds are generally hotter than the flesh, so leave them in if you like your food hot. Wash your hands, knife, and chopping board thoroughly before preparing any other ingredients or touching your eyes or face.

Thai and Chinese cooks also make use of dried chilies. Normally the seeds are left in and the chilies can be used either whole, split lengthwise or crushed. They can also be rehydrated in almost boiling water before use. The chilies are usually removed from the dish before serving.

CHILI BEAN SAUCE

This is a thick sauce or paste made from soy beans, chilies, and other seasonings and is usually hot and spicy. It is available in jars from supermarkets and Asian grocery stores and keeps well in the refrigerator.

CHILI SAUCE

This is a bright red, hot sauce made from chilies, vinegar, sugar, and salt. It is sometimes used in cooking but is mainly useful as a dipping sauce. It is also available as sweet chili sauce.

COCONUT

Coconut is a very common ingredient in Thai cooking. It is available in many forms including fresh, dried, powdered, creamed, and in cans. Recipes generally specify which type to use.

CILANTRO (CHINESE PARSLEY)

Fresh, green cilantro is used extensively in Thai cooking and is one of the few fresh herbs used in Chinese cookery. The leaves resemble those of Italian parsley and the two are easily confused, although cilantro has a much more pungent flavor and aroma. Cilantro is often sold in bunches with the roots still attached. The roots are also often used in Thai recipes, especially for curry pastes. Coriander seeds are used whole or ground and are also most often used to make curry pastes.

CORNSTARCH

Cornstarch is a very common thickening agent in Chinese cooking but is also used in marinades to coat food and protect it during deep-frying. To create a sauce with a velvety texture, mix the cornstarch with a little water until smooth, then add to the sauce in the wok and heat gently, stirring throughout.

FISH SAUCE

This is the basic savory flavor in Thai cooking for which there is no substitute. It is made from fermented fish or seafood and imparts a very distinctive, salty flavor. Fish sauce is readily available in large supermarkets and Asian grocery stores.

GARLIC

Both Chinese and Thai cuisine rely on garlic as an essential seasoning. It is used in many forms. It is often pickled or used to flavor oils and sauces and is often paired with other pungent ingredients such as scallions, ginger, and black beans. Look for firm, pinkish garlic and store in a cool, dry place.

GINGER AND GALANGAL

Fresh ginger is an indispensable ingredient in Chinese cooking, although it is also used in some Thai dishes. Ginger has a pungent, fresh, spicy fragrance and adds a subtle, hot flavor to dishes. Galangal is similar but is more often used in Thai cooking.

HOISIN SAUCE

This is a thick, brownish-red sauce made from soy beans, vinegar, sugar, and spices. It is sweet and spicy and is widely used in Chinese cookery. It is probably best known as an accompaniment to Peking Duck. It should keep indefinitely in the refrigerator.

KAFFIR LIME LEAVES

The dark green, glossy leaves of the Kaffir lime impart a unique, lemon-lime flavor to Thai cooking. They are used whole in soups and stews or finely sliced in stir-fried dishes. They are readily available in Asiab grocery stores and some supermarkets. Buy a large bunch and freeze in plastic containers—they will keep indefinitely. They are also available dried but are less pungent this way.

LEMON GRASS

A common Thai ingredient, lemon grass looks a little like the scallion. It is much tougher, however, and has a pungent lemony flavor (but lemon is not a good substitute). To use lemon grass, trim the ends, remove the toughest outer leaves and chop finely.

OIL

Oil is the most common cooking medium in wok cookery, although other fats can be used. The most common oil to use is peanut oil. It is virtually tasteless and has a high smoke point, making it ideal for both stir-frying and deep-frying. Another suitable oil is corn oil. Do not use olive oil or any of the nut oils for stir-frying, as these oils have a tendency to burn at low temperatures.

Sesame oil is a thick, rich, pungent oil made from toasted sesame seeds. In Chinese cooking, it is used as a seasoning and is added after cooking. It heats very quickly and burns very easily, making it unsuitable for cooking.

RICE VINEGAR

There are several types of rice vinegar, ranging in flavor from spicy and slightly tart to sweet and pungent. White rice vinegar is the most common and is clear and mild in flavor. It is used for sweet and sour dishes. Black rice vinegar is dark in color. It is rich yet mild in flavor and is used in braised dishes and sauces. Red rice vinegar is sweet and spicy and is usually used as a dipping sauce for seafood.

RICE WINE

Look for Shaoxing or Shaoxing-style rice wine as it has a rich, mellow flavor that is unique. A reasonable substitute is dry sherry; it is not expensive and keeps well in the pantry.

SOY SAUCE

The most essential ingredient in Chinese cooking, soy sauce is made from a mixture of soy beans, flour, and water, which is then fermented and aged for some months. The liquid, which is finally distilled is soy sauce. There are two main types: light soy sauce and dark soy sauce. Light soy sauce, which is light in color but very flavorful, is best for cooking. (It is saltier than dark soy sauce.) Dark soy sauce is aged for longer than light soy sauce and has a darker, almost black color. It is slightly thicker and stronger than light soy sauce and is generally used as a dipping sauce. Japanese soy sauce is also very dark but has a more rounded flavor, while still being salty.

TAMARIND

A useful sour flavor in Thai cooking, tamarind is usually available in compressed blocks from Asian grocery stores. To extract the juice or water, mix the pulp with double the amount of hot water, then press through a strainer. Discard the seeds.

TOFU

Tofu is also known by its Chinese name doufu. It is an important ingredient in both Thai and Chinese cuisines and is highly nutritious, being rich in protein. It has a distinctive texture but very bland flavor. It is made from yellow soy beans that have been soaked, ground, mixed with water and then cooked briefly before being solidified. It is sold in several forms; some varieties are coarse-textured, whereas others are silky and smooth. The coarser type is useful for stir-frying, while the silky type is often used in soups.

Tofu is usually sold packaged in water. Once opened, store in the refrigerator for up to five days, changing the water daily. To use solid tofu, drain it well by pressing between sheets of absorbent paper towels and then cut into cubes or shreds. Cook it carefully as too much handling will cause it to disintegrate.

EQUIPMENT AND TECHNIQUES

There are numerous pieces of equipment that are very useful for stir-frying. Most can be bought very cheaply from Asian grocery stores, or often more expensively from department stores.

EQUIPMENT

WOK

The most useful piece of equipment is, of course, the wok. It is much easier to use than a skillet because of its depth, making it easier to toss the food around quickly without spilling it. A wok also requires a lot less oil for deep-frying than a deep-fat fryer, although more care is required in terms of safety. Another advantage is that the shape of the wok allows heat to spread more evenly, ensuring that the food cooks much more quickly.

There are a number of shapes of wok available. The Cantonese wok has short handles on each side. This type of wok is best for steaming and deep-frying because it is easier to move when full of liquid. The Pau wok has a single handle and is better for stir-frying, allowing you to maneuver the wok with one hand while stirring the food with the other one.

Woks can also have rounded or flattened bottoms. Round-bottomed woks are suitable for use on gas burners. Flattened-bottomed woks can be used on gas and electric burners but are better for deep-frying than stir-frying.

When choosing a wok, look for a large one simply because it is easier to cook a small amount in a large wok than a large amount in a small one. Choose a wok that is heavy and made of carbon steel, rather than stainless steel or aluminum, which tend to scorch. Nonstick woks are also available but these cannot be seasoned or used over very high temperatures, both of which are essential for flavor in stir-frying. Electric woks are also available but these cannot be heated sufficiently hot enough and tend to have very shallow sides. They also lack the maneuvrability of a free-standing wok.

If you buy a carbon-steel wok, it will need to be seasoned before use. First, scrub well using a cream cleanser or another abrasive to remove the machine oil with which it will probably have been coated to prevent rusting. Dry it well and then place it over a low heat. Add a little cooking oil and rub this all over the cooking surface with wadded paper towels. Continue heating over a low heat for 10–15 minutes, then wipe well with more paper towels—the paper will blacken. Repeat this process of coating, heating, and wiping until the paper towel comes away clean. With continued use, the wok will darken further.

Do not scrub a seasoned wok with soap and water. Wash in hot, plain water using a brush or nonstick scrubber. Dry thoroughly with absorbent paper towels and place over a low heat until completely dry. Rub with a few drops of cooking oil to prevent rusting. If a little rust does appear, scrub off with cream cleanser or another abrasive and repeat the seasoning process.

ACCESSORIES

If your burner will not support a free-standing wok, Asian stores sell metal rings or frames, called wok stands, that stabilize round-bottomed woks. These stands are an essential piece of equipment, so if you plan on doing a lot of steaming, deep-frying or braising in your wok it may be worth purchasing one. The stands are available in two designs: one is a solid ring punched with ventilation holes and the other is a circular wire frame. Only use the wire frame stand if you have a gas burner as the other stand will not allow sufficient ventilation.

You may also find it useful to have a lid for your wok. Wok lids are domelike in shape, are usually made from aluminum and are very inexpensive. Any large, dome-shaped saucepan lid that fits snugly over the wok will suffice. Alternatively, use aluminum foil.

A long-handled spatula is also an important piece of equipment. Special spatulas with rounded ends are readily available and make stirring and tossing food in the wok much easier. A long-handled spoon can be used instead.

If you are going to use the wok as a steamer, a wooden or metal rack or trivet is also a useful tool, as it holds the plate or steamer above the water.

Chinese cooks would not be without a cleaver. It differs from a meat cleaver in that a Chinese cleaver has a finer, much sharper blade and is used for all kinds of cutting, from shredding to chopping up bones. Several types of Chinese cleavers are available including a lightweight, narrow-bladed cleaver for cutting delicate foods such as vegetables, a medium-weight model for general use and a heavy cleaver for heavy duty chopping.

For steaming, it may be worth investing in a bamboo steamer. They are both attractive and effective. They come in a variety of sizes and stack together with the uppermost basket having a lid. Fill the steamer with food, placing the food needing the longest cooking time in the bottom basket and the more delicate foods in the top basket. Stand the steamer on a trivet in a steady wok of boiling water. Cover tightly and let cook.

Another useful piece of equipment if you plan to do a lot of cooking in the wok is an electric rice cooker. It will cook rice perfectly and keep it warm, sometimes up to several hours. It also has the advantage of freeing-up cooker space. They are relatively expensive, however but if you cook rice frequently it may be worth buying.

Chopsticks are used in Chinese and Japanese cookery not just for eating but for stirring, beating, and whipping. They are available in wood and plastic and can be bought in Asian grocery stores and also department stores. Chinese chopsticks are larger with blunted ends, while Japanese chopsticks tend to be smaller with pointed ends.

To use chopsticks, put one chopstick into the crook of your preferred hand, between your thumb and index finger, holding the chopstick about two thirds of the way up from the thinner end. Let it rest on your third finger. Put the second chopstick between your thumb and index finger so that its tip is level with the chopstick below. Keep the lower chopstick steady and move the top one to pick up food.

TECHNIQUES

The initial preparation of food in wok cooking is probably more important than the cooking itself. Most dishes are cooked very rapidly, so it is important that everything is prepared beforehand and is chopped into small, even-sized pieces to ensure quick, even cooking without overcooking. This type of preparation also ensures the dish looks attractive.

Wok cookery covers a number of different cooking methods—sometimes in one recipe—and most are easily mastered. When planning a meal, make sure you select dishes using different cooking methods and only one that is stir-fried.

CUTTING TECHNIQUES

SLICING Several different types of slicing methods are useful in wok and stir-fry cooking, including the conventional method of laying the food firmly on a chopping board and slicing straight down to cut the food into thin slices. Meat is always sliced across the grain to break up the fibers and to make it more tender when cooked. If you use a cleaver, hold the cleaver with your index finger over the far side of the top of the cleaver and your thumb on the side nearest to you and guide the cutting edge firmly through the food. With your other hand, hold the food and make sure when cutting that you turn your fingers under for safety.

CHOPPING This is the simplest technique and refers to simply cutting food through. With whole birds or cooked food with bones, which needs to be chopped into smaller pieces, place on a firm surface, then using a straight, sharp, downward motion, chop through the bones, hitting down with the blade, then finish off the blow with the flat of your other hand on the top edge of the knife or cleaver. A heavy cleaver or knife is best for these tasks.

DIAGONAL SLICING This is particularly useful for vegetables as it exposes more surface area to the heat of the wok and also makes the food look much more interesting. Simply angle the knife or cleaver against the food and slice. For larger vegetables such as zucchini, carrots, and eggplants, make one diagonal cut at the end of the vegetable. Turn the vegetable ninety degrees, cut in half lengthwise, then diagonally slice each half. Continue until the whole vegetable has been chopped into even-sized pieces.

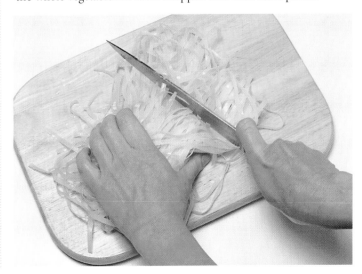

DICING This is a simple technique of cutting food into small cubes or dice. First cut the food into slices as for shredding. Stack the slices and slice again lengthwise into sticks, again as you would for shredding. Turn the sticks again and cut crosswise into cubes.

HORIZONTAL OR FLAT SLICING

This is a technique for slicing whole foods thinly, while retaining the overall shape. A cleaver is particularly useful for this technique. Hold the knife or cleaver with the blade parallel to the chopping board. Place your free hand on top of the food to be sliced. Using a gentle slicing motion, slice sideways into the food and right the way through, taking care to keep your upper hand out of the way. This is particularly useful for splitting chicken breasts and similar meats.

MINCING This is a very fine chopping technique. First slice the food and then chop it rapidly—it will spread out over the chopping area. Gather it into a pile and continue chopping and regathering until the food is chopped as finely as needed. If very fine results are required, a food processor may be a better tool to use but be careful not to overprocess.

SCORING This is used to score the surface of foods, such as duck breasts and squid to help them cook faster and evenly and to give them an attractive appearance. Use a cleaver or sharp knife and make shallow cuts into the food at a slight angle. Take care not to cut all the way through. Make cuts right across the food, then turn and make a second series of cuts at an angle to the first set to make diamond shapes.

SHREDDING This is cutting food into fine, matchstick shreds. First cut the food into slices, then stack the slices and cut again, lengthwise this time, into fine shreds. It is sometimes easier to cut meat and fish if they have been placed in the freezer for 20–30 minutes before slicing.

OTHER USEFUL TECHNIQUES

MARINATING This is a common process in Chinese and other Asian cookery to add flavor to meat, fish, and vegetables. The food is steeped in a mixture of flavors, which could include soy sauce, rice wine, garlic, ginger or spices. Marinating time is usually at least 20 minutes but often can be as long as overnight. Food is usually removed from the marinade before cooking.

THICKENING There are two useful ways of thickening sauces. The first is to use cornstarch mixed until smooth with a little water that is then beaten into the hot, not boiling, sauce. The sauce is brought up to simmer and cooked gently for about 2 minutes until thickened. The other method of thickening is to reduce the sauce; the liquid is simmered until most of the excess liquid has boiled off, leaving a concentrated and thickened sauce.

VELVETING This is a particularly useful technique in Chinese cooking, which helps to protect delicate foods, such as chicken breasts, from overcooking. The food is coated with a mixture of cornstarch and egg white, and sometimes salt. The mixture is marinated in the refrigerator for 20–30 minutes before cooking.

COOKING TECHNIQUES

BLANCHING This method involves cooking food in boiling water or moderately hot oil for a few minutes so that it is partly cooked, which speeds up the cooking process later on, so that other elements of the dish do not overcook. Chicken is often blanched in oil after velveting, meat is often blanched in water to remove excess fat and vegetables are often blanched in water, drained and refreshed under cold water, before being drained again and dried. In the case of vegetables, stir-frying merely heats them through and finishes the cooking.

BRAISING This is a method often applied to tougher cuts of meat that need long, slow cooking times to remain moist. The food is usually browned and then cooked in stock or liquid to which other flavorings are also added. The mixture is brought up to simmering point and then cooked gently until tender.

DEEP-FRYING This is another very important technique in Far Eastern cookery. Woks are very useful for deep-frying as they use far less oil than conventional deep-fat fryers. Although a deep-fat fryer is safer, a few precautions mean that deep-frying in a wok is very easy. Ensure that the wok sits securely on the burner, either by using a flat-bottomed wok or a wok stand. Carefully add the oil, ensuring that the wok is no more than half full. Heat up slowly to the required temperature.

To test for temperature, either use a thermometer made for the purpose or the following test. Add a small cube of crustless bread and time how long it takes to brown. Generally, if the bread browns in 30 seconds, the oil is at the correct temperature. If it browns more quickly the oil is too hot. If it takes longer to brown the oil is too cold. Let the oil return to the correct temperature between batches of food and do not overfill the wok. Do not leave the wok unsupervised when deep frying.

It is also important that food to be deep-fried is dry. Lift food from a marinade and blot thoroughly on paper towels. If using batter, allow any excess to drip off before adding to the oil.

Oil used for deep-frying can be reused. Let the oil cool completely and then strain into a clean jar or other container. Label the jar with the type of food the oil was used for and only reuse it for the same type of food. Oil can be reused up to three times.

PAN-FRYING This is similar to sautéing as it involves more oil than stir-frying but less than deep-frying. Food is fried first on one side and then on the other. Often the excess oil is drained off and a sauce is made in the same saucepan. A skillet is preferable for pan-frying rather than a wok.

POACHING This is a method of cooking meat or fish in simmering liquid until nearly cooked so that it can be added to soup or combined with a sauce to finish the cooking.

SLOW-SIMMERING AND STEEPING Slow-simmered food is cooked very gently in liquid that just simmers. Simmering is the method for making stock. Steeping is a similar method, except that the heat is turned off and the heat of the liquid alone finishes off the cooking process.

STEAMING Steaming is an ancient technique currently enjoying a revival because it adds no fat to the food being cooked. Steamed foods are cooked on a gentle, moist heat. Steaming is particularly suited to vegetable and fish.

Woks can be used as steamers in two ways. The first method is described under the section on bamboo steamers. The second method involves putting about 2 inches (5 cm) of water in a stable wok on the burner. A metal or wooden rack or trivet is then placed into the wok and the water is brought to a boil. The food to be steamed should be arranged on a plate and the plate should be lowered onto the rack. The wok then needs to be covered tightly with a lid. For longer cooking times, the water may need replenishing.

STIR-FRYING This is the most famous of wok cooking techniques and is used throughout China and the Far East as well as in India. It is possibly the most tricky of wok techniques because it involves a lot of preparation as well as a good source of heat. Its advantage is that stir-fried foods can be cooked very quickly in very little oil so that they retain their color, flavor, and texture. It is very important that stir-fried foods are not greasy or overcooked.

STEPS TO STIR-FRYING (ONCE ALL THE INGREDIENTS ARE PREPARED AND TO HAND):

- Heat the wok or skillet over the highest heat until it is very hot before adding the oil. This prevents the food from sticking and also ensures an even heat. Add the oil and using a spatula or long-handled spoon, distribute it evenly over the surface. It should be very hot—almost smoking—before you add any ingredients (unless you are adding flavoring ingredients). If you are flavoring the oil, for example with some chopped garlic, ginger, scallions or chili (or a combination) do not let the oil become smoking hot because these types of ingredients

will burn at such high temperatures and become bitter. Add to hot but not smoking oil and toss the ingredients around quickly for a few seconds. In some recipes these ingredients are removed and discarded.

- Now add the next ingredients as described in the recipe and proceed to stir-fry by tossing quickly in the wok using a spatula or long-handled spoon. When cooking meat, let it rest for a few seconds between stirring it. Otherwise keep the food moving, transferring it from the bottom to the sides of the wok and back again. Because of the high heat involved when stir-frying, there may be some spluttering and splattering of hot fat, so take care during this stage of cooking.

- Once everything is cooked, some stir-fried dishes are thickened with a mixture of cornstarch and water. To avoid a lumpy sauce, make sure the mixture is smooth and reduce the heat to just below simmering point before adding it. Stir in the cornstarch mixture, then increase the heat to a simmer and cook for an additional 2–3 minutes until the sauce is thickened, smooth, and coats all the ingredients.

TWICE COOKING As the name implies, this is a two step process involving two different techniques, such as simmering and stir-frying. For example, pork ribs may be gently simmered to remove the excess fat before draining and stir-frying or braising with other flavors.

GARNISHES

Asian cuisines pay a lot of attention to the finished appearance of food and this is one reason for cutting ingredients carefully. Often dishes will be garnished attractively with anything from simple shredded chilies to more elaborate scallion tassels. Thai cooks often go to elaborate lengths, carving flowers from carrots or making tomato roses as garnishes. In fact, the Thai Royal family employs an official Fruit Carver (a hereditary post) for special occasions. The home cook can create some simple effects with everyday ingredients and a sharp knife.

CHILI FLOWERS Take a well-formed red chili, about 2–3 inches (5–7.5 cm) long, with the stem intact. Hold the chili by the stem and, using a fine sharp knife, cut from the tip to the stem, at equal distances all the way around, without cutting through the stem. Try to leave the seeds intact. Gently pull back the strips and drop into iced water. The strips will curl back into a flower.

SCALLION TASSELS Trim the top green end of a scallion and cut a piece about 2–3 inches (5–7.5 cm) long, including about ½ inch (1 cm) of the white base. With a fine, sharp knife, and holding the white part as a base, shred the green part as finely as possible. Drop into a bowl of iced water until the shreds curl back.

WON TON SOUP

INGREDIENTS   Serves 6

FOR THE CHICKEN STOCK:

2 lb. (900 g) chicken or chicken
   pieces with back, feet, and
   wings
1–2 onions, peeled and
   quartered
2 carrots, peeled and chopped
2 celery stalks, trimmed and
   chopped
1 leek, trimmed and chopped
2 garlic cloves, unpeeled and
   lightly crushed
1 tbsp. black peppercorns
2 bay leaves
1 small bunch parsley, stems
   only

2–3 slices fresh ginger, peeled
   (optional)
3½ quarts (3.4 liters) cold water

FOR THE SOUP:

18 won tons
2–3 Chinese cabbage, or a
   handful of spinach, shredded
1 small carrot, peeled and cut
   into matchsticks
2–4 scallions, trimmed and
   diagonally sliced
soy sauce, to taste
handful Italian parsley, to
   garnish

1 Chop the chicken into
6–8 pieces and put into
a large stock pot or saucepan
of water with the remaining
stock ingredients. Place over
a high heat and bring to a
boil, skimming off any scum
that rises to the surface.
Reduce the heat and simmer
for 2–3 hours, skimming
occasionally.

2 Strain the stock through a
fine strainer or cheesecloth-
lined strainer into a large bowl.
Let cool, then chill in the
refrigerator for 5–6 hours or
overnight. When cold, skim off
the fat and remove any small
pieces of fat by dragging a piece
of absorbent paper towels lightly
across the surface.

3 Bring a medium saucepan
of water to a boil. Add
the won tons and return to a
boil. Simmer for 2–3 minutes
or until the won tons are cooked,
stir frequently. Rinse under
cold running water, drain
and set aside.

4 Pour 1¼ cups stock per
person into a large wok.
Bring to a boil over a high heat,
skimming any foam that rises to
the surface and simmer for 5–7
minutes to reduce slightly. Add
the won tons, Chinese cabbage
or spinach, carrots, and scallions.
Season with a few drops of
soy sauce and simmer for 2–3
minutes. Garnish with a few
Italian parsley leaves and serve
immediately.

THAI HOT-&-SOUR SHRIMP SOUP

INGREDIENTS   Serves 6

1½ lb. (700 g) large raw shrimp
2 tbsp. vegetable oil
3–4 stalks lemon grass, outer
  leaves discarded and
  coarsely chopped
1 in. (2.5 cm) piece fresh
  ginger, peeled and finely
  chopped
2–3 garlic cloves, peeled and
  crushed
small bunch fresh cilantro,
  leaves stripped and
  set aside, stems finely
  chopped

½ tsp. freshly ground black
  pepper
6 cups water
1–2 small red chilies, seeded
  and thinly sliced
1–2 small green chilies,
  seeded and thinly sliced
6 kaffir lime leaves, thinly
  shredded
4 scallions, trimmed and
  diagonally sliced
1–2 tbsp. Thai fish sauce
1–2 tbsp. freshly squeezed
  lime juice

1 Remove the heads from the shrimp by twisting away from the body and set aside. Shell the shrimp, leaving the tails on and set aside the shells with the heads. Using a sharp knife, remove the black vein from the back of the shrimp. Rinse and dry the shrimp and set aside. Rinse and dry the heads and shells.

2 Heat a wok, add the oil and, when hot, add the shrimp heads and shells, the lemon grass, ginger, garlic, cilantro stems, and black pepper and stir-fry for 2–3 minutes or until the shrimp heads and shells turn pink and all the ingredients are colored.

3 Carefully add the water to the wok and return to a boil, skimming off any scum that rises to the surface. Simmer over a medium heat for 10 minutes or until slightly reduced. Strain through a fine strainer and return the clear shrimp stock to the wok.

4 Bring the stock back to a boil and add the reserved shrimp, chilies, lime leaves, and scallions and simmer for 3 minutes or until the shrimp turn pink. Season with the fish sauce and lime juice. Spoon into heated soup bowls, dividing the shrimp evenly and float a few cilantro leaves over the surface.

FOOD FACT

Thai fish sauce, made from fermented anchovies, has a sour, salty, fishy flavor.

CREAMY CARIBBEAN CHICKEN & COCONUT SOUP

INGREDIENTS   Serves 4

6–8 scallions

2 garlic cloves

1 red chili

2 cups cooked chicken, shredded or diced

2 tbsp. vegetable oil

1 tsp. ground turmeric

1 cup coconut milk

3 cups chicken stock

½ cup small soup pasta or spaghetti, broken into small pieces

½ lemon, sliced

salt and freshly ground black pepper

1–2 tbsp. freshly chopped cilantro

sprigs of fresh cilantro, to garnish

1 Trim the scallions and thinly slice; peel the garlic and finely chop. Cut off the top from the chili, slit down the side and remove seeds and membrane, then finely chop and set aside.

2 Remove and discard any skin or bones from the cooked chicken and shred using two forks and set aside.

3 Heat a large wok, add the oil and, when hot, add the scallions, garlic, and chili and stir-fry for 2 minutes or until the scallions have softened. Stir in the turmeric and cook for 1 minute.

4 Blend the coconut milk with the chicken stock until smooth, then pour into the wok. Add the pasta or spaghetti with the lemon slices and bring to a boil.

5 Simmer, half covered, for 10–12 minutes or until the pasta is tender; stir occasionally.

6 Remove the lemon slices from the wok and add the chicken. Season to taste with salt and pepper and simmer for 2–3 minutes or until the chicken is heated through thoroughly.

7 Stir in the chopped cilantro and ladle into heated bowls. Garnish with sprigs of fresh cilantro and serve immediately.

HELPFUL HINT

Be careful handling chilies. Either wear rubber gloves or scrub your hands thoroughly, using plenty of soap and water. Avoid touching eyes or any other sensitive areas.

CORN & CRAB SOUP

INGREDIENTS   Serves 4

1 lb. (450 g) fresh corn-on-the-cob

5 cups chicken stock

2–3 scallions, trimmed and finely chopped

½ in. (1 cm) piece fresh ginger, peeled and finely chopped

1 tbsp. dry sherry or Chinese rice wine

2–3 tsp. soy sauce

1 tsp. light brown sugar

salt and freshly ground black pepper

2 tsp. cornstarch

½ lb. (225 g) white crabmeat, fresh or canned

1 medium egg white

1 tsp. sesame oil

1–2 tbsp. freshly chopped cilantro

1 Wash the corn cobs and dry. Using a sharp knife and holding the corn cobs at an angle to the cutting board, cut down along the cobs to remove the kernels, then scrape the cobs to remove any excess milky residue. Put the kernels and the milky residue into a large wok.

2 Add the chicken stock to the wok and place over a high heat. Bring to a boil, stirring and pressing some of the kernels against the side of the wok to squeeze out the starch to help thicken the soup. Simmer for 15 minutes, stirring occasionally.

3 Add the scallions, ginger, sherry or Chinese rice wine, soy sauce, and brown sugar to the wok and season to taste with salt and pepper. Simmer for an additional 5 minutes, stirring occasionally.

4 Blend the cornstarch with 1 tablespoon of cold water to form a smooth paste and beat into the soup. Return to a boil, then simmer over a medium heat until thickened.

5 Add the crabmeat, stirring until blended. Beat the egg white with the sesame oil and stir into the soup in a slow steady stream, stirring constantly. Stir in the chopped cilantro and serve immediately.

TASTY TIP

For chicken stock that is homemade, follow the instructions for Won Ton Soup (see page 16).

Hot-&-Sour Soup

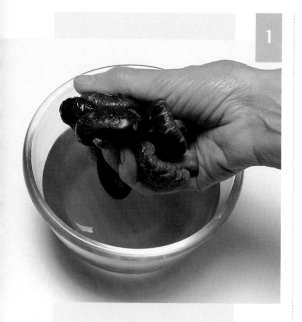

INGREDIENTS
Serves 4–6

¼ cup dried Chinese (shiitake) mushrooms

2 tbsp. peanut oil

1 carrot, peeled and cut into julienne strips

1 cup chestnut or brown mushrooms, wiped and thinly sliced

2 garlic cloves, peeled and finely chopped

½ tsp. dried crushed chilies

5 cups chicken stock (see page 16)

1 cup cooked boneless chicken or pork, shredded

½ cup fresh beancurd or tofu, thinly sliced (optional)

2–3 scallions, trimmed and finely diagonally sliced

1–2 tsp. sugar

3 tbsp. vinegar

2 tbsp. soy sauce

salt and freshly ground black pepper

1 tbsp. cornstarch

1 large egg

2 tsp. sesame oil

2 tbsp. freshly chopped cilantro

1 Place the dried Chinese (shiitake) mushrooms in a small bowl and pour over enough almost boiling water to cover. Leave for 20 minutes to soften, then gently lift out and squeeze out the liquid. (Lifting out the mushrooms leaves any sand and grit behind.) Discard the stems and thinly slice the caps and set aside.

2 Heat a large wok, add the oil and when hot, add the carrot strips and stir-fry for 2–3 minutes or until beginning to soften. Add the chestnut mushrooms and stir-fry for 2–3 minutes or until golden, then stir in the garlic and chilies.

3 Add the chicken stock to the vegetables and bring to a boil, skimming any foam that rises to the surface. Add the shredded chicken or pork, beancurd, if using, scallions, sugar, vinegar, soy sauce and reserved Chinese mushrooms. Simmer for 5 minutes, stirring occasionally. Season to taste with salt and pepper.

4 Blend the cornstarch with 1 tablespoon of cold water to form a smooth paste and beat into the soup. Return to a boil and simmer over a medium heat until thickened.

5 Beat the egg with the sesame oil and slowly add to the soup in a slow, steady stream, stirring constantly. Stir in the chopped cilantro and serve the soup immediately.

CHINESE CABBAGE & MUSHROOM SOUP

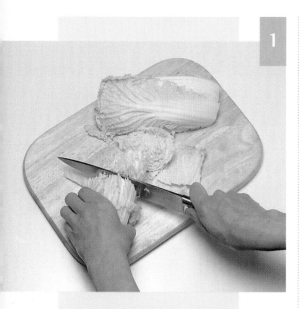

INGREDIENTS   Serves 4–6

1 lb. (450 g) Chinese cabbage
¼ cup dried Chinese
  (shiitake) mushrooms
1 tbsp. vegetable oil
⅓ cup bacon, diced
1 in. (2.5 cm) piece fresh
  ginger, peeled and finely
  chopped
1½ cups chestnut or brown
  mushrooms, thinly sliced

5 cups chicken stock
4–6 scallions, trimmed and cut
  into short lengths
2 tbsp. dry sherry or Chinese
  rice wine
salt and freshly ground black
  pepper
sesame oil for drizzling

1 Trim the stem ends of the Chinese cabbage and cut in half lengthwise. Remove the triangular core, then cut into 1 inch (2.5 cm) slices and set aside.

2 Place the dried Chinese mushrooms in a bowl and pour over enough almost boiling water to cover. Let stand for 20 minutes to soften, then gently lift out and squeeze out the liquid. Discard the stems and thinly slice the caps and set aside. Strain the liquid through a cheesecloth-lined strainer and set aside.

3 Heat a wok over a medium high heat, add the oil and, when hot, add the bacon. Stir-fry for 3–4 minutes or until crisp and golden, stirring frequently. Add the ginger and chestnut mushrooms and stir-fry for an additional 2–3 minutes.

4 Add the chicken stock and bring to a boil, skimming any fat and scum that rises to the surface. Add the scallions, sherry or rice wine, Chinese cabbage, sliced Chinese mushrooms, and season to taste with salt and pepper. Pour in the reserved soaking liquid and reduce the heat to the lowest possible setting.

5 Simmer gently, covered until all the vegetables are very tender; this will take about 10 minutes. Add a little water if the liquid has reduced too much. Spoon into soup bowls and drizzle with a little sesame oil. Serve immediately.

TASTY TIP

If Chinese cabbage is not available, use bok choy.

VIETNAMESE BEEF & RICE NOODLE SOUP

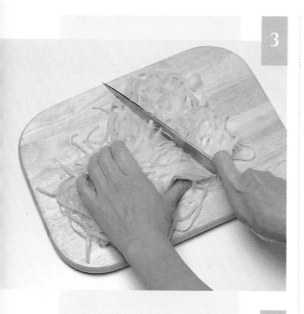

INGREDIENTS   Serves 4–6

FOR THE BEEF STOCK:
2 lb. (900 g) meaty beef bones
1 large onion, peeled and
  quartered
2 carrots, peeled and cut
  into chunks
2 celery stalks, trimmed and
  sliced
1 leek, washed and sliced
  into chunks
2 garlic cloves, unpeeled and
  lightly crushed
3 whole star anise
1 tsp. black peppercorns

FOR THE SOUP:
2½ cups dried rice stick
  noodles
4–6 scallions, trimmed and
  diagonally sliced
1 red chili, seeded and
  diagonally sliced
1 small bunch fresh
  cilantro
1 small bunch fresh mint
¾ lb. (350 g) fillet steak, very
  thinly sliced
salt and freshly ground black
  pepper

1 Place all the ingredients for the beef stock into a large stock pot or saucepan and cover with cold water. Bring to a boil and skim off any scum that rises to the surface. Reduce the heat and simmer gently, partially covered for 2–3 hours, skimming occasionally.

2 Strain into a large bowl and let cool, then skim off the fat. Chill in the refrigerator and when cold remove any fat from the surface. Pour 6 cups of the stock into a large wok and set aside.

3 Cover the noodles with warm water and leave for 3 minutes or until just softened. Drain, then cut into 4 inch (10 cm) lengths.

4 Arrange the scallions and chili on a serving platter or large serving plate. Strip the leaves from the cilantro and mint and then arrange them in piles on the plate.

5 Bring the stock in the wok to a boil over a high heat. Add the noodles and simmer for about 2 minutes or until tender. Add the beef strips and simmer for about 1 minute. Season to taste with salt and pepper.

6 Ladle the soup with the noodles and beef strips into individual soup bowls and serve immediately with the plate of condiments handed around separately.

LAKSA MALAYAN RICE NOODLE SOUP

INGREDIENTS　　　　　　　Serves 4–6

2½ lb. (1.1 kg) corn-fed,
　free-range chicken
1 tsp. black peppercorns
1 tbsp. vegetable oil
1 large onion, peeled and
　thinly sliced
2 garlic cloves, peeled and
　finely chopped
1 in. (2.5 cm) piece fresh
　ginger, peeled and thinly
　sliced
1 tsp. ground coriander
2 red chilies, seeded and
　diagonally sliced

1–2 tsp. hot curry paste
1½ cups coconut milk
1 lb. (450 g) large raw shrimp,
　shelled and veined
½ small head of Chinese
　cabbage, thinly shredded
1 tsp. sugar
2 scallions, trimmed and
　thinly sliced
¾ cup beansprouts
3½ cups rice noodles or rice
　sticks, soaked as per
　package instructions
fresh mint leaves, to garnish

1 Put the chicken in a large saucepan with the peppercorns and cover with cold water. Bring to a boil, skimming off any scum that rises to the surface. Simmer, partially covered for about 1 hour. Remove the chicken and cool. Skim any fat from the stock and strain through a cheesecloth-lined strainer and set aside. Remove the meat from the carcass, shred, and set aside

2 Heat a large wok, add the oil and, when hot, add the onions and stir-fry for 2 minutes or until they begin to color. Stir in the garlic, ginger, coriander, chilies, and curry paste and stir-fry for an additional 2 minutes.

3 Carefully pour in the reserved stock (you need at least 5 cups) and simmer gently, partially covered for 10 minutes or until slightly reduced.

4 Add the coconut milk, shrimp, Chinese cabbage, sugar, scallions, and beansprouts and simmer for 3 minutes, stirring occasionally. Add the reserved shredded chicken, and cook for an additional 2 minutes.

5 Drain the noodles and divide among 4–6 soup bowls. Ladle the hot stock and vegetables over the noodles, making sure each serving has some shrimp and chicken. Garnish each bowl with fresh mint leaves and serve immediately.

WOK-FRIED SNACKS—POPCORN & SESAME-COATED PECANS

INGREDIENTS Serves 4–6

FOR THE POPCORN:
6 tbsp. vegetable oil
½ cup unpopped popcorn
½ tsp. garlic salt
1 tsp. hot chili powder

FOR THE PECANS:
1 cup sugar
½ tsp. ground cinnamon

½ tsp. ground Chinese five
spice powder
¼ tsp. salt
¼ tsp. cayenne pepper
1½ cups pecan or walnut
halves
sesame seeds for sprinkling

1 For the popcorn, heat half the oil in a large wok over a medium high heat. Add 2–3 kernels and cover with a lid. When these kernels pop, add all the popcorn and cover tightly. Cook until the popping stops, shaking from time to time.

2 When the popping stops, pour the popped corn into a bowl and immediately add the remaining oil to the wok with the garlic salt and chili powder. Stir-fry for 30 seconds or until blended and fragrant.

3 Return the popcorn to the wok, stir-fry and toss for an additional 30 seconds or until coated. Pour into the bowl and serve warm.

4 For the pecans, put the sugar, cinnamon, Chinese five spice powder, salt, and cayenne pepper into a large wok

and stir in ¼ cup water. Bring to a boil over a high heat, then simmer for 4 minutes, stirring frequently.

5 Remove from the heat and stir in the pecans or walnuts until well coated. Turn onto a lightly greased, nonstick baking tray and sprinkle generously with the sesame seeds.

6 Working quickly with two forks, separate the nuts into individual pieces or bite-sized clusters. Sprinkle with a few more sesame seeds and let cool completely. Carefully remove from the baking tray, breaking into smaller pieces if necessary.

HELPFUL HINT

Popping corn is readily available and should be stored in an airtight container.

SHRIMP TOASTS

INGREDIENTS

Serves 8–10

2 cups cooked shelled shrimp, thawed if frozen, well drained, and dried

1 medium egg white

2 scallions, trimmed and chopped

½ in. (1 cm) piece fresh ginger, peeled and chopped

1 garlic clove, peeled and chopped

1 tsp. cornstarch

2–3 dashes hot pepper sauce

½ tsp. sugar

salt and freshly ground black pepper

8 slices firm-textured white bread

4–5 tbsp. sesame seeds

1 cup vegetable oil for deep frying

sprigs of fresh cilantro, to garnish

1 Put the shrimp, egg white, scallions, ginger, garlic, cornstarch, hot pepper sauce, and sugar into a food processor. Season to taste with about ½ teaspoon of salt and black pepper.

2 Process until the mixture forms a smooth paste, scraping down the sides of the bowl once or twice.

3 Using a metal palette knife, spread an even layer of the paste evenly over the bread slices. Sprinkle each slice generously with sesame seeds, pressing gently to bury them in the paste.

4 Trim the crusts off each slice, then cut each slice diagonally into 4 triangles. Cut each triangle in half again to make 8 pieces from each slice.

5 Heat the vegetable oil in a large wok to 375° F (190° C)

or until a small cube of bread browns in about 30 seconds. Working in batches, deep-fry the shrimp triangles for 30–60 seconds or until they are golden, turning once.

6 Remove with a slotted spoon and drain on absorbent paper towels. Keep the toasts warm. Arrange them on a large serving plate and garnish with sprigs of fresh cilantro Serve immediately.

TASTY TIP

This is a classic Chinese appetizer. Serve it with a selection of other snacks as a starter or with drinks.

SESAME SHRIMP

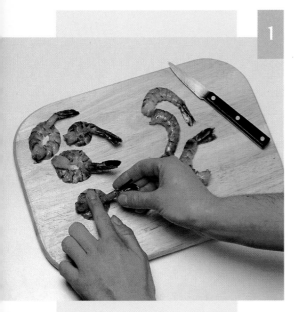

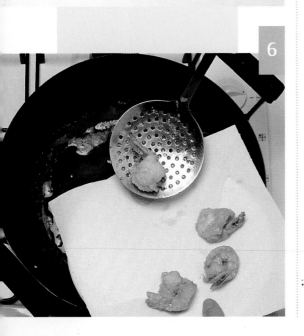

INGREDIENTS

Serves 6–8

24 large raw shrimp
¼ cup all-purpose
  flour
4 tbsp. sesame seeds
salt and freshly ground black
  pepper
1 large egg
1 cup vegetable oil
  for deep-frying

FOR THE SOY DIPPING SAUCE:
¼ cup soy sauce
1 scallion, trimmed and finely
  chopped
½ tsp. dried crushed chilies
1 tbsp. sesame oil
1–2 tsp. sugar, or to taste
strips of scallion,
  to garnish

1 Remove the heads from the shrimp by twisting away from the body and discard. Shell the shrimp, leaving the tails on for presentation. Using a sharp knife, remove the black vein from the back of the shrimp. Rinse and dry.

2 Slice along the back but do not cut through the shrimp body. Place on the chopping board and press firmly to flatten slightly, to make a butterfly shape.

3 Put the flour, half the sesame seeds, salt, and pepper into a food processor and blend for 30 seconds. Tip into a plastic bag or a plastic container and add the shrimp, 4–5 at a time. Mix to coat with the flour.

4 Beat the egg in a small bowl with the remaining sesame seeds, salt, and pepper.

5 Heat the oil in a large wok to 375° F (190° C) or until a small cube of bread browns in

about 30 seconds. Working in batches of five or six, and holding each shrimp by the tail, dip into the beaten egg, then carefully lower into the oil.

6 Cook for 1–2 minutes or until crisp and golden, turning once or twice. Using a slotted spoon, remove the shrimp, drain on absorbent paper towels and keep warm.

7 To make the dipping sauce, stir together the soy sauce, scallion, chilies, oil, and sugar until the sugar dissolves. Arrange the shrimp on a plate, garnish with strips of scallion and serve immediately.

HELPFUL HINT

Raw shrimp are widely available but are cheapest bought frozen in boxes from Asian grocery stores.

SPRING ROLLS

INGREDIENTS — Makes 26–30 rolls

FOR THE FILLING:

2 tbsp. dried Chinese (shiitake) mushrooms
1 cup rice vermicelli
1–2 tbsp. peanut oil
1 small onion, peeled and finely chopped
3–4 garlic cloves, peeled and finely chopped
1½ in. (4 cm) piece fresh ginger, peeled and chopped
1 cup fresh ground pork
2 scallions, trimmed and finely chopped
1 cup beansprouts
4 water chestnuts, chopped
2 tbsp. freshly snipped chives
1½ cups cooked shelled shrimp, chopped
1 tsp. oyster sauce
1 tsp. soy sauce
salt and freshly ground black pepper
scallion tassels, to garnish

FOR THE WRAPPERS:

4–5 tbsp. all-purpose flour
26–30 spring roll wrappers
1 cup vegetable oil for deep-frying

1 Soak the Chinese mushrooms in almost boiling water for 20 minutes. Remove and squeeze out the liquid. Discard any stems, slice and set aside. Soak the rice vermicelli as package instructions.

2 Heat a large wok and, when hot, add the oil. Heat, then add the onion, garlic, and ginger and stir-fry for 2 minutes.

3 Add the pork, scallions, and Chinese mushrooms and stir-fry for 4 minutes. Stir in the beansprouts, water chestnuts, chives, shrimp, oyster, and soy sauce. Season to taste with salt and pepper and spoon into a bowl.

4 Drain the noodles well, add to the bowl and toss until well mixed, then let cool.

5 Blend the flour to a smooth paste with 3–4 tablespoons of water. Soften a wrapper in a plate of warm water for 1–2 seconds, then drain. Put 2 tablespoons of the filling near one edge of the wrapper, fold the edge over the filling, then fold in each side and roll up. Seal with a little flour paste and transfer to a baking tray, seam side down. Repeat with the remaining wrappers.

6 Heat the oil in a large wok to 375° F (190° C) or until a cube of bread browns in 30 seconds. Deep-fry the spring rolls a few at a time until golden. Remove and drain on paper towels. Arrange on a serving plate and garnish with scallion tassels. Serve immediately.

BARBECUE PORK STEAMED BUNS

INGREDIENTS   Serves 12

FOR THE BUNS:
1½–1¾ cups all-purpose flour
1 tbsp. rapid rise active dry
   yeast
½ cup milk
2 tbsp. corn oil
1 tbsp. sugar
½ tsp. salt
scallion tassels,
   to garnish
fresh green salad leaves,
   to serve

FOR THE FILLING:
2 tbsp. vegetable oil
1 small red bell pepper,
   seeded and finely chopped
2 garlic cloves, peeled and
   finely chopped
2½ cups cooked pork, finely
   chopped
¼ cup firmly packed light
   brown sugar
¼ cup tomato ketchup
1–2 tsp. hot chili powder

1 Put ¾ cup of the flour in a bowl and stir in the yeast. Heat the milk, oil, sugar, and salt in a small saucepan until warm, stirring until the sugar has dissolved. Pour into the bowl and, with an electric mixer, beat on a low speed for 30 seconds, scraping down the sides of the bowl until blended. Beat at high speed for 3 minutes, then with a wooden spoon, stir in as much of the remaining flour as possible, until a stiff dough forms. Shape into a ball, place in a greased bowl, cover with plastic wrap and leave for 1 hour in a warm place or until doubled in size.

2 To make the filling, heat a wok, add the oil and, when hot, add the red bell pepper and garlic. Stir-fry for 4–5 minutes. Add the remaining ingredients and bring to a boil, stir-frying for 2–3 minutes until thick and syrupy. Cool and set aside.

3 Punch down the dough and turn onto a lightly floured surface. Divide into 12 pieces and shape them into balls, then cover and let rest for 5 minutes.

4 Roll each ball to a 3 inch (7.5 cm) circle. Place a heaped tablespoon of filling in the center of each. Dampen the edges, then bring them up and around the filling, pinching together to seal. Place seam side down on a small square of nonstick parchment paper. Continue with remaining dough and filling. Let rise for 10 minutes.

5 Bring a large wok half filled with water to a boil, place the buns in a lightly greased Chinese steamer, without touching each other. Cover and steam for 20–25 minutes, then remove and cool slightly. Garnish with scallion tassels and serve with salad leaves.

CHICKEN-FILLED SPRING ROLLS

INGREDIENTS

Makes 12–14 rolls

FOR THE FILLING:
1 tbsp. vegetable oil
2 slices bacon, diced
½ lb. (225 g) skinless
   chicken breast fillets,
   thinly sliced
1 small red bell pepper,
   seeded and finely chopped
4 scallions, trimmed and finely
   chopped
1 in. (2.5 cm) piece fresh
   ginger, peeled and finely
   chopped
¾ cup snow peas, thinly sliced

¾ cup beansprouts
1 tbsp. soy sauce
2 tsp. Chinese rice wine or dry
   sherry
2 tsp. hoisin or plum sauce

FOR THE WRAPPERS:
3 tbsp. all-purpose flour
12–14 spring roll wrappers
1 cup vegetable oil for
   deep-frying
shredded scallions,
   to garnish
dipping sauce, to serve

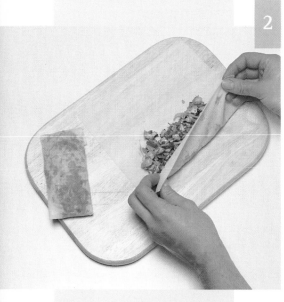

1 Heat a large wok, add the oil and, when hot, add the diced bacon and stir-fry for 2–3 minutes or until golden. Add the chicken and bell pepper and stir-fry for an additional 2–3 minutes. Add remaining filling ingredients and stir-fry 3–4 minutes until the vegetables are tender. Turn into a strainer and let drain as the mixture cools.

2 Blend the flour with about 1½ tablespoons of water to form a paste. Soften each wrapper in a plate of warm water for 1–2 seconds, then place on a chopping board. Put 2–3 tablespoons of filling on the near edge. Fold the edge over the filling to cover. Fold in each side and roll up. Seal the edge with a little flour paste and press to seal securely. Transfer to a baking tray, seam side down.

3 Heat the oil in a large wok to 375° F (190° C) or until a small cube of bread browns in about 30 seconds. Working in batches of 3–4, deep-fry the spring rolls until they are crisp and golden, turning once (about 2 minutes). Remove and drain on absorbent paper towels. Arrange the spring rolls on a serving plate, garnish with scallion tassels and serve hot with dipping sauce.

HELPFUL HINT

As always with wok cooking, it is important to cut all the ingredients into uniform small pieces. This will ensure that everything cooks quickly but will also make the spring rolls easier to roll.

FRIED PORK-FILLED WON TONS

INGREDIENTS   Makes 24

FOR THE FILLING:
3 cups cooked pork, finely
  chopped
2–3 scallions, trimmed and
  finely chopped
1 in. (2.5 cm) piece fresh
  ginger, grated
1 garlic clove, peeled and
  crushed
1 small egg, lightly beaten
1 tbsp. soy sauce
1 tsp. light brown sugar
1 tsp. sweet chili sauce or
  tomato ketchup
24–30 won ton wrappers,
  3½ inches (8 cm) square
1 cup vegetable oil for
  deep-frying

**FOR THE GINGER DIPPING
  SAUCE:**
4 tbsp. soy sauce
1–2 tbsp. rice or raspberry
  vinegar
1 in. (2.5 cm) piece fresh
  ginger, peeled and finely
  slivered
1 tbsp. sesame oil
1 tbsp. light brown sugar
2–3 dashes hot chili sauce
scallion tassels, to garnish

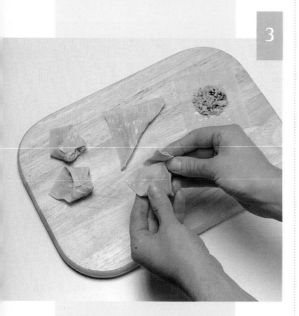

1 Place all the filling
ingredients into a
food processor and, using
the pulse button, process
until well blended. Do not
overwork, the filling should
have a coarse texture.

2 Lay out the won ton
wrappers on a chopping
board and put a teaspoon of the
filling in the center of each.

3 Brush the edges with water
and bring up two opposite
corners of each square over the
filling to form a triangle, pressing
the edges firmly to seal. Dampen
the two other corners and overlap
them slightly, pressing firmly to

seal, to form an oven-envelope
shape, similar to a tortellini.

4 For the dipping sauce, stir
together all the ingredients
until the sugar is dissolved. Pour
into a serving bowl and set aside.

5 Heat the oil in a large wok to
375° F (190° C) or until a
small cube of bread browns in
about 30 seconds.

6 Working in batches of 5–6,
deep-fry until the won tons
are crisp and golden, turning
once or twice. Remove and drain
on paper towels. Garnish with
scallion tassels and serve hot with
the dipping sauce.

Shrimp Salad with Toasted Rice

INGREDIENTS   Serves 4

FOR THE DRESSING:
¼ cup rice vinegar
1 red chili, seeded and thinly
   sliced
3 in. (7.5 cm) piece lemon
   grass stalk, bruised
1 tbsp. lime juice
2 tbsp. Thai fish sauce
1 tsp. sugar, or to taste

FOR THE SALAD:
¾ lb. (350 g) large raw shrimp,
   shelled with tails attached,
   heads removed

cayenne pepper
1 tbsp. long-grain white rice
salt and freshly ground black
   pepper
2 tbsp. corn oil
1 large head Chinese cabbage
   or romaine lettuce, shredded
½ small cucumber,
   peeled, seeded and
   thinly sliced
1 small bunch chives, cut into
   1 in. (2.5 cm) pieces
small bunch mint leaves

1 Place all the ingredients for the dressing in a small bowl and let stand to allow the flavors to blend together.

2 Using a sharp knife, split each shrimp lengthwise in half, leaving the tail attached to one half. Remove any black vein and pat the shrimp dry with absorbent paper towels. Sprinkle the shrimp with a little salt and cayenne pepper and then set aside.

3 Heat a wok over a high heat. Add the rice and stir-fry until browned and fragrant. Turn into a mortar and cool. Crush gently with a pestle until coarse crumbs form. Wipe the wok clean.

4 Reheat the wok, add the oil and, when hot, add the shrimp and stir-fry for 2 minutes or until pink. Transfer to a plate and season to taste with salt and pepper.

5 Place the Chinese cabbage or lettuce into a salad bowl with the cucumber, chives, and mint leaves and toss lightly together.

6 Remove the lemon grass stalk and some of the chili from the dressing and pour all but 2 tablespoons over the salad and toss until lightly coated. Add the shrimp and drizzle with the remaining dressing, then sprinkle with the toasted rice and serve.

STICKY BRAISED SPARE RIBS

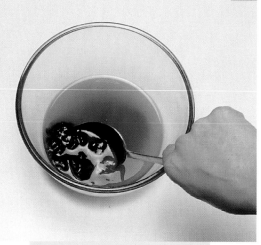

INGREDIENTS   Serves 4

2 lb. (900 g) meaty pork spare
  ribs, cut crosswise into
  3 in. (7.5 cm) pieces
½ cup orange juice
¼ cup dry white wine
3 tbsp. black bean sauce
3 tbsp. tomato ketchup
2 tbsp. honey
3–4 scallions, trimmed and
  chopped
2 garlic cloves, peeled and
  crushed

1 tbsp. grated orange zest
salt and freshly ground black
  pepper

TO GARNISH:
scallion tassels
lemon wedges

1 Put the spare ribs in the wok
and add enough cold water
to cover. Bring to a boil over a
medium high heat, skimming
any scum that rises to the surface.
Cover and simmer for 30 minutes,
then drain and rinse the ribs.

2 Rinse and dry the wok and
return the ribs to it. In a
bowl, blend the orange juice with
the white wine, black bean sauce,
tomato ketchup, and the honey
until smooth.

3 Stir in the scallions,
crushed garlic cloves,
and the grated orange zest. Stir
well until mixed thoroughly.

4 Pour the mixture over the
spare ribs in the wok and stir
gently until the ribs are lightly
coated. Place over a moderate
heat and bring to a boil.

5 Cover, then simmer, stirring
occasionally for 1 hour or
until the ribs are tender and the
sauce is thickened and sticky.
(If the sauce reduces too quickly
or begins to stick, add water 1
tablespoon at a time until the ribs
are tender.) Adjust the seasoning
to taste, then transfer the ribs to a
serving plate and garnish with
scallion tassels and lemon
wedges. Serve immediately.

HELPFUL HINT

It's probably best to get your
butcher to cut the ribs into
pieces for you, as they are
quite bony. Boiling the ribs
before cooking them in the
sauce reduces the fat content
and ensures that they are
tender and more succulent.

SOY-GLAZED CHICKEN THIGHS

INGREDIENTS

Serves 6–8

2 lb. (900 g) chicken thighs
2 tbsp. vegetable oil
3–4 garlic cloves, peeled and crushed
1½ in. (4 cm) piece fresh ginger, peeled and finely chopped or grated
½ cup soy sauce

2–3 tbsp. Chinese rice wine or dry sherry
2 tbsp. honey
1 tbsp. brown sugar
2–3 dashes hot chili sauce, or to taste
freshly chopped parsley, to garnish

1 Heat a large wok and, when hot, add the oil and heat. Stir-fry the chicken thighs for 5 minutes or until golden. Remove and drain on absorbent paper towels. You may need to do this in 2–3 batches.

2 Pour off the oil and fat and, using absorbent paper towels, carefully wipe out the wok. Add the garlic, with the ginger, soy sauce, Chinese rice wine or sherry, and honey to the wok and stir well. Sprinkle in the brown sugar with the hot chili sauce to taste, then place over the heat and bring to a boil.

3 Reduce the heat to a gentle simmer, then carefully add the chicken thighs. Cover the wok and simmer gently over a very low heat for 30 minutes or until they are tender and the sauce is reduced and thickened and glazes the chicken thighs.

4 Stir or spoon the sauce occasionally over the chicken thighs and add a little water if the sauce is starting to become too thick. Arrange in a shallow serving dish, garnish with freshly chopped parsley and serve immediately.

TASTY TIP

Often overlooked, chicken wings are inexpensive and very flavorful. Served this way, with a sticky coating, they make an ideal snack. Serve with finger bowls.

SHREDDED DUCK IN LETTUCE LEAVES

INGREDIENTS   Serves 4–6

2 tbsp. dried Chinese (shiitake) mushrooms

2 tbsp. vegetable oil

1 lb. (450 g) boneless, skinless duck breast, cut crosswise into thin strips

1 red chili, seeded and diagonally thinly sliced

4–6 scallions, trimmed and diagonally sliced

2 garlic cloves, peeled and crushed

¾ cup beansprouts

3 tbsp. soy sauce

1 tbsp. Chinese rice wine or dry sherry

1–2 tsp. honey or brown sugar

4–6 tbsp. hoisin or plum sauce

large, crisp lettuce leaves such as romaine

handful of fresh mint leaves

dipping sauce (see Sesame Shrimp, page 36)

1 Cover the dried Chinese mushrooms with almost boiling water, leave for 20 minutes, then drain and slice thinly.

2 Heat a large wok, add the oil and, when hot, stir-fry the duck for 3–4 minutes or until sealed. Remove with a slotted spoon and set aside.

3 Add the chili, scallions, garlic, and Chinese mushrooms to the wok and stir-fry for 2–3 minutes or until softened.

4 Add the beansprouts, the soy sauce, Chinese rice wine or dry sherry, and honey or brown sugar to the wok, and continue to stir-fry for 1 minute, or until blended.

5 Stir in the reserved duck and stir-fry for 2 minutes or until well mixed together and heated right through. Transfer to a heated serving dish.

6 Arrange the hoisin sauce in a small bowl on a tray or plate with a pile of lettuce leaves and the mint leaves.

7 Let each guest spoon a little hoisin sauce onto a lettuce leaf, then top with a large spoonful of the stir-fried duck and vegetables and roll up the leaf to enclose the filling. Serve with the dipping sauce.

FOOD FACT

Hoisin sauce is a sweet and spicy aromatic Chinese sauce made primarily from soy beans, sugar, garlic, and chili.

SWEDISH COCKTAIL MEATBALLS

INGREDIENTS   Serves 4–6

½ stick butter
1 onion, peeled and finely
  chopped
½ cup fresh white bread
  crumbs
1 medium egg, beaten
½ cup heavy cream
salt and freshly ground black
  pepper

1½ cups fresh lean ground
  beef
½ cup fresh ground pork
3–4 tbsp. freshly chopped dill
½ tsp. ground allspice
1 tbsp. vegetable oil
½ cup beef stock
cream cheese and chive or
  cranberry sauce, to serve

1 Heat half the butter in a large wok, add the onion and cook, stirring frequently for 4–6 minutes or until softened and beginning to color. Transfer to a bowl and let cool. Wipe out the wok with absorbent paper towels.

2 Add the bread crumbs and beaten egg with 1–2 tablespoons of cream to the softened onion. Season to taste with salt and pepper and stir until well blended. Using your fingertips crumble the ground beef and pork into the bowl.

3 Add half the dill, the allspice and, using your hands, mix together until well blended. With dampened hands, shape the mixture into 1 inch (2.5 cm) balls.

4 Melt the remaining butter in the wok and add the vegetable oil, swirling it to coat the sides of the wok.

5 Working in batches, add about one quarter to one third of the meatballs in a single layer and cook for 5 minutes, swirling and turning until golden and cooked.

6 Transfer to a plate and continue with the remaining meatballs, transferring them to the plate as they are cooked.

7 Pour off the fat in the wok. Add the beef stock and bring to a boil, then boil until reduced by half, stirring and scraping up any browned bits from the bottom. Add the remaining cream and continue to simmer until slightly thickened and reduced.

8 Stir in the remaining dill and season if necessary. Add the meatballs and simmer for 2–3 minutes or until heated right through. Serve with toothpicks, with the sauce in a separate bowl for dipping.

FRESH TUNA SALAD

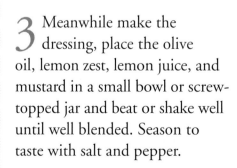

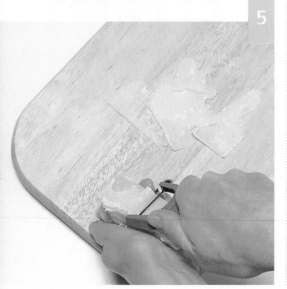

INGREDIENTS

Serves 4

5 cups mixed salad leaves

2 cups baby cherry tomatoes, halved lengthwise

2½ cups arugula, washed

2 tbsp. peanut oil

1¼ lb. (550 g) boned tuna steaks, each cut into 4 small pieces

small piece fresh Parmesan cheese

FOR THE DRESSING:

½ cup olive oil

1 tbsp. grated lemon zest

2 tbsp. lemon juice

1 tbsp. mustard

salt and freshly ground black pepper

1 Wash the salad leaves and place in a large salad bowl with the cherry tomatoes and arugula and set aside.

2 Heat the wok, then add the oil and heat until almost smoking. Add the tuna, skin side down, and cook for 4–6 minutes, turning once during cooking or until cooked and the flesh flakes easily. Remove from the heat and let stand in the juices for 2 minutes before removing.

3 Meanwhile make the dressing, place the olive oil, lemon zest, lemon juice, and mustard in a small bowl or screw-topped jar and beat or shake well until well blended. Season to taste with salt and pepper.

4 Transfer the tuna to a clean chopping board and flake, then add it to the salad and toss lightly.

5 Using a swivel blade vegetable peeler, peel the piece of Parmesan cheese into shavings. Divide the salad among 4 large serving plates, drizzle the dressing over the salad, then sprinkle with the Parmesan shavings.

HELPFUL HINT

Bags of mixed salad leaves are available from all major supermarkets. Although they seem expensive, there is very little waste and they do save time. Rinse the leaves before using.

SALMON NOISETTES WITH FRUITY SAUCE

INGREDIENTS   Serves 4

4 salmon steaks
2 tbsp. grated lemon rind
¼ cup lemon juice
2 tsp. grated lime rind
1 tbsp. lime juice
3 tbsp. olive oil
1 tbsp. honey
1 tbsp. mustard
coarse sea salt and freshly
  ground black pepper
1 tbsp. peanut oil

2½ cups mixed salad leaves,
  washed
1 bunch watercress, washed
  and thick stalks removed
2¼ cups baby plum
  tomatoes, halved

1 Using a sharp knife, cut the bone away from each salmon steak to create 2 salmon fillets. Repeat with the remaining salmon steaks. Shape the salmon fillets into noisettes and secure with kitchen string.

2 Mix together the citrus rinds and juices, olive oil, honey, mustard, salt, and pepper in a shallow dish. Add the salmon fillets and turn to coat. Cover and allow to marinate in the refrigerator for about 4 hours, turning them occasionally in the marinade.

3 Heat the wok, then add the peanut oil and heat until hot. Lift out the salmon noisettes, setting the marinade aside. Add the salmon to the wok and cook for 6–10 minutes, turning once during cooking until cooked and the fish is just flaking. Pour the marinade into the wok and heat through gently.

4 Mix together the salad leaves, watercress, and tomatoes and arrange on serving plates. Top with the salmon noisettes and drizzle over any remaining warm marinade. Serve immediately.

HELPFUL HINT

When choosing salad leaves for this dish, look out for slightly bitter leaves such as Italian red lettuce and radicchio, which will stand up well to the heat of the salmon and contrast with the sweetness of the sauce.

SALMON WITH STRAWBERRY SAUCE

INGREDIENTS

Serves 4

4 salmon fillets
¼ stick butter
2 tbsp. peanut oil
1 eating apple, cored and cut into chunks
1 bunch scallions, trimmed and diagonally sliced
1 garlic clove, peeled and sliced
½ cup pine nuts

2 tbsp. lemon juice
1 cup strawberries, hulled and halved
1 bunch basil, freshly chopped
salt and freshly ground black pepper

TO SERVE:
freshly cooked creamy mashed potatoes
freshly cooked fava beans

1 Wash the salmon fillets and pat dry on absorbent paper towels. Heat the wok, then add the butter and half the oil and heat until bubbling. Cook the salmon fillets flesh side down for 5 minutes until they are sealed. Then, using a spatula, carefully turn the salmon fillets over and cook for an additional 3–5 minutes until the salmon flesh is just flaking.

2 Transfer the salmon fillets to warmed serving plates and keep warm in a low oven. Wipe the wok clean, then add the remaining oil to the wok and heat until almost smoking.

3 Add the apple chunks, scallions, garlic slices, and pine nuts and cook for about 5 minutes, stirring occasionally until they are golden brown.

4 Stir in the lemon juice, strawberries, chopped basil, and season to taste with salt and pepper. Heat through thoroughly.

5 Spoon the sauce over the salmon fillets and serve immediately with creamy mashed potatoes and freshly cooked fava beans.

HELPFUL HINT

This unusual fruit sauce provides a much needed sharpness against the richness of the fish. Do not overcook the strawberries, however, or they will lose their shape and texture.

STIR-FRIED JUMBO SHRIMP

INGREDIENTS — Serves 4

1¼ cups fine egg thread
  noodles
1¼ cups broccoli florets
1¼ cups baby corn, halved
3 tbsp. soy sauce
1 tbsp. lemon juice
pinch of sugar
1 tsp. chili sauce
1 tsp. sesame oil
2 tbsp. corn oil
1 lb. (450 g) raw jumbo
  shrimp, shelled, heads
  and tails removed,
  and veined

1 in. (2.5 cm) piece fresh
  ginger, peeled and cut into
  sticks
1 garlic clove, peeled and
  chopped
1 red chili, seeded and sliced
2 medium eggs, lightly beaten
8 oz. (225 g) can water
  chestnuts, drained and sliced

1 Place the noodles in a large bowl, cover with plenty of boiling water and let stand for 5 minutes or according to the package directions; stir occasionally. Drain and set aside. Blanch the broccoli and corn in a saucepan of boiling salted water for 2 minutes, then drain and set aside.

2 Meanwhile, mix together the soy sauce, lemon juice, sugar, chili sauce, and sesame or vegetable oil in a bowl and set aside.

3 Heat a large wok, then add the corn oil and heat until just smoking. Add the jumbo shrimp and stir-fry for 2–3 minutes or until pink on all sides. Using a slotted spoon, transfer the shrimp to a plate and set aside. Add the ginger and stir-fry for 30 seconds. Add the garlic and chili to the wok and cook for an additional 30 seconds.

4 Add the noodles and stir-fry for 3 minutes until the noodles are crisp. Stir in the shrimp, vegetables, eggs, and water chestnuts and stir-fry for an additional 3 minutes until the eggs are lightly cooked. Pour over the chili sauce, stir lightly and serve immediately.

HELPFUL HINT

Egg noodles are available in a variety of thicknesses. All are very quick to cook and are an excellent pantry ingredient.

CREAMY MIXED SEAFOOD WITH SPAGHETTI

INGREDIENTS   Serves 4

4 cups spaghetti

2 tbsp. peanut oil

1 bunch scallions, trimmed and diagonally sliced

1 garlic clove, peeled and chopped

1 cup frozen peas

1½ cups shelled shrimp, thawed if frozen

¼ cucumber, peeled if preferred and chopped

⅔ cup dry vermouth or white wine

½ cup heavy cream

14 oz. (400 g) can salmon, drained, boned, skinned, and flaked

pinch of paprika

salt and freshly ground black pepper

½ cup freshly shredded Parmesan cheese (optional)

1 Bring a large saucepan of salted water to a boil and add the spaghetti. Bring back to a boil and cook at a rolling boil for 8 minutes or until "al dente." Drain thoroughly.

2 Meanwhile heat a large wok, then add the oil and heat until almost smoking. Stir-fry the scallions for 2 minutes, then add the garlic and peas and stir-fry for 3 minutes.

3 Add the shrimp and stir-fry for 2 minutes until heated through and browned slightly. Add the cucumber and cook for 2 minutes.

4 Stir in the vermouth or white wine and bring to a boil. Simmer for 3 minutes until reduced and thickened slightly.

Add the cream, stirring until well blended, then add the salmon and paprika. Bring almost to a boil, toss in the pasta and cook until heated through. Season to taste with salt and pepper, add the Parmesan cheese, if desired and serve immediately.

TASTY TIP

Choose canned red salmon for this recipe, rather than the cheaper pink salmon. The flavor is fuller and the texture is also better. If you don't like cleaning canned fish you can buy it skinned and boned.

COCONUT SEAFOOD

INGREDIENTS   Serves 4

2 tbsp. peanut oil
1 lb. (450 g) raw jumbo
  shrimp, shelled
2 bunches scallions,
  trimmed and thickly
  sliced
1 garlic clove, peeled and
  chopped
1 in. (2.5 cm) piece fresh
  ginger, peeled and cut into
  matchsticks

1 cup fresh shiitake
  mushrooms, rinsed and
  halved
⅔ cup dry white wine
1 cup coconut cream
4 tbsp. freshly chopped
  cilantro
salt and freshly ground
  black pepper
freshly cooked Thai
  fragrant rice

1 Heat a large wok, add the oil and heat until it is almost smoking, swirling the oil around the wok to coat the sides. Add the shrimp and stir-fry over a high heat for 4-5 minutes or until browned on all sides. Using a slotted spoon, transfer the shrimp to a plate and keep warm in a low oven.

2 Add the scallions, garlic, and ginger to the wok and stir-fry for 1 minute. Add the mushrooms and stir-fry for an additional 3 minutes. Using a slotted spoon, transfer the mushroom mixture to a plate and keep warm in a low oven.

3 Add the wine and coconut cream to the wok, bring to a boil and boil rapidly for 4 minutes until reduced slightly.

4 Return the mushroom mixture and shrimp to the wok, bring back to a boil, then simmer for 1 minute, stirring occasionally until piping hot. Stir in the freshly chopped cilantro and season to taste with salt and pepper. Serve immediately with the freshly cooked Thai fragrant rice.

HELPFUL HINT

If coconut cream is not available, shred ½ cup creamed coconut into ¾ cup hot water. Beat until completely dissolved and use as above.

LOBSTER & SHRIMP CURRY

INGREDIENTS   Serves 4

2½ cups cooked lobster meat,
  shelled if necessary
½ lb. (225 g) raw jumbo
  shrimp, shelled and veined
2 tbsp. peanut oil
2 bunches scallions,
  trimmed and thickly
  sliced
2 garlic cloves, peeled and
  chopped
1 in. (2.5 cm) piece fresh
  ginger, peeled and cut into
  matchsticks
2 tbsp. Thai red curry paste

2 tsp. grated lime zest
1 tbsp. lime juice
1 cup coconut cream
salt and freshly ground black
  pepper
3 tbsp. freshly chopped
  cilantro
freshly cooked Thai fragrant
  rice, to serve

1 Using a sharp knife, slice the lobster meat thickly. Wash the jumbo shrimp and pat dry with absorbent paper towels. Make a small ½ inch (1 cm) cut at the tail end of each shrimp and set aside.

2 Heat a large wok, then add the oil and, when hot, stir-fry the lobster and jumbo shrimp for 4–6 minutes or until pink. Using a slotted spoon, transfer to a plate and keep warm in a low oven.

3 Add the scallions and stir-fry for 2 minutes, then stir in the garlic and ginger and stir-fry for an additional 2 minutes. Add the curry paste and fry for 1 minute.

4 Pour in the coconut cream, lime zest, lime juice, and the

seasoning. Bring to a boil and simmer for 1 minute. Return the shrimp and lobster and any juices to the wok and simmer for 2 minutes. Stir in two thirds of the freshly chopped cilantro to the wok mixture, then sprinkle with the remaining cilantro and serve immediately.

FOOD FACT

This dish is not as expensive
as it first appears, since
one small lobster is easily
enough for 4 people.

Smoked Salmon with Fava Beans & Rice

INGREDIENTS   Serves 4

2 tbsp. corn oil

¼ stick unsalted butter

1 onion, peeled and chopped

2 garlic cloves, peeled and chopped

¾ cup asparagus tips, halved

1 cup frozen fava beans

⅔ cup dry white wine

½ cup sundried tomatoes, drained and sliced

2½ cups baby spinach leaves, washed

5 cups cooked long-grain rice

3 tbsp. sour cream

½ lb. (225 g) smoked salmon, cut into strips

¾ cup freshly shredded Parmesan cheese

salt and freshly ground black pepper

1 Heat a large wok, then add the oil and butter and, when melted, stir-fry the onion for 3 minutes until almost softened. Add the garlic and asparagus tips and stir-fry for 3 minutes. Add the fava beans and wine and bring to a boil, then simmer, stirring occasionally until the wine is reduced slightly.

2 Add the sundried tomatoes and bring back to a boil, then simmer for 2 minutes. Stir in the baby spinach leaves and cooked rice and return to a boil. Stir-fry for 2 minutes or until the spinach is wilted and the rice is heated through thoroughly.

3 Stir in the sour cream, smoked salmon strips and Parmesan cheese. Stir well and cook, stirring frequently until piping hot. Season to taste with salt and pepper. Serve immediately.

HELPFUL HINT

To make 5 cups cooked rice, measure ¾ cup long-grain rice. Wash well in several changes of water and drain. Put into a saucepan with enough cold water to cover the rice by about 1 inch (2.5 cm), add salt and stir well. Bring to a boil over a high heat, then reduce the heat to very low, cover and cook for 10 minutes. Remove from the heat and leave, covered for an additional 10 minutes. Do not lift the lid until the full 20 minutes have elapsed.

SPECIAL FRIED RICE

INGREDIENTS   Serves 4

pat of butter
4 medium eggs, beaten
4 tbsp. peanut oil
1 bunch scallions, trimmed
   and finely shredded
1¼ cups cooked ham, diced
¾ lb. (350 g) large cooked
   shrimp, thawed if frozen
   and shelled
1 cup peas, thawed
   if frozen

5 cups cooked long-grain rice
2 tbsp. dark soy sauce
1 tbsp. sherry
salt and freshly ground black
   pepper
1 tbsp. freshly torn
   cilantro

1 Heat a wok, lightly grease with the butter and when melted, pour in half the beaten eggs. Cook for 4 minutes, stirring frequently until the egg has set, forming an omelet. Using a spatula, lift the omelet from the wok and roll up into a sausage shape. When cool, using a sharp knife, slice the omelet into thin rings, then set aside.

2 Wipe the wok clean with absorbent paper towels and heat it. Add the oil and heat until just smoking. Add the shredded scallions, the ham, shrimp, and peas and stir-fry for 2 minutes or until heated through thoroughly. Add the cooked rice and stir-fry for an additional 2 minutes.

3 Stir in the remaining beaten eggs and stir-fry for 3 minutes or until the egg has set. Stir in the soy sauce and sherry, and season to taste with salt and

pepper, then heat until piping hot. Add the omelet rings and gently stir through the mixture, making sure not to break up the omelet rings. Sprinkle with the freshly torn cilantro and serve immediately.

HELPFUL HINT

Use cold cooked rice (see Helpful Hint in previous recipe for cooking) as it is less likely to stick to the wok. Make sure, however, that the rice is heated right through and is piping hot. Do not reheat more than once and never keep cooked rice longer than 24 hours.

CHILI ANGLER FISH STIR FRY

INGREDIENTS   Serves 4

4½ cups pasta twists
1¼ lb. (550 g) angler fish,
    trimmed and cut into chunks
2 tbsp. peanut oil
1 green chili, seeded
    and cut into matchsticks
2 tbsp. sesame seeds
pinch of cayenne pepper
sliced green chilies,
    to garnish

FOR THE MARINADE:
1 garlic clove, peeled and
    chopped
2 tbsp. dark soy sauce
2 tsp. grated lime zest
1 tbsp. lime juice
1 tbsp. sweet chili sauce
¼ cup olive oil

1 Bring a large saucepan of lightly salted water to a boil and add the pasta. Stir, bring back to a boil and cook at a rolling boil for 8 minutes or until "al dente." Drain thoroughly and set aside.

2 For the marinade, mix together the sliced garlic, dark soy sauce, lime zest, lime juice, sweet chili sauce, and olive oil in a shallow dish, then add the angler fish chunks. Stir until all the angler fish is lightly coated in the marinade, then cover and leave in the refrigerator for at least 30 minutes, spooning the marinade over the fish occasionally.

3 Heat a wok, then add the oil and heat until almost smoking. Remove the angler fish from the marinade, scraping off as much marinade as possible, add to the wok and stir-fry for 3 minutes. Add the green chili and sesame seeds and stir-fry for an additional 1 minute.

4 Stir in the pasta and marinade and stir-fry for 1–2 minutes or until piping hot. Sprinkle with cayenne pepper and garnish with sliced green chilies. Serve immediately.

HELPFUL HINT

Although a fish merchant will bone the angler fish, it is very simple to do. Clean the fish of any skin or membrane. With a large sharp knife, feel for the bone that runs down the center of the fish. Keeping the knife as close to the bone as possible, cut down the length of the fish on either side of the bone to remove the fillets.

TERIYAKI SALMON

INGREDIENTS   Serves 4

1 lb. (450 g) salmon fillet,
  skinned
6 tbsp. Japanese teriyaki
  sauce
1 tbsp. rice wine vinegar
1 tbsp. tomato paste
dash of Tabasco sauce
2 tsp. grated lemon zest

salt and freshly ground black
  pepper
¼ cup peanut oil
1 carrot, peeled and cut into
  matchsticks
1 cup snow peas
1¾ cups oyster or exotic
  mushrooms, wiped

1 Using a sharp knife, cut the salmon into thick slices and place in a shallow dish. Mix together the teriyaki sauce, rice wine vinegar, tomato paste, Tabasco sauce, lemon zest, and seasoning. Spoon the marinade over the salmon, then cover loosely and allow to marinate in the refrigerator for 30 minutes, turning the salmon or spooning the marinade occasionally over the salmon.

2 Heat a large wok, then add 2 tablespoons of the oil until almost smoking. Stir-fry the carrot for 2 minutes, then add the snow peas and stir-fry for an additional 2 minutes. Add the mushrooms and stir-fry for 4 minutes until softened. Using a slotted spoon, transfer the vegetables to 4 warmed serving plates and keep warm.

3 Remove the salmon from the marinade, setting aside both the salmon and marinade. Add the remaining oil to the wok,

heat until almost smoking, then cook the salmon for 4–5 minutes, turning once during cooking or until the fish is just flaking. Add the marinade and heat through for 1 minute. Serve immediately with the salmon arranged on top of the vegetables and the marinade drizzled over.

TASTY TIP

Teriyaki sauce is available readymade but to make your own, mix together 2 tablespoons sake, 2 tablespoons mirin, 2 tablespoons Japanese soy sauce and 2 tablespoons sugar. Beat together until the sugar has dissolved and use as above.

GOUJONS OF FLOUNDER WITH TARTARE SAUCE

INGREDIENTS   Serves 4

¾ cup fresh white
  bread crumbs
3 tbsp. freshly shredded
  Parmesan cheese
salt and freshly ground black
  pepper
1 tbsp. dried oregano
1 medium egg
1 lb. (450 g) flounder fillets
1 cup vegetable oil for
  deep frying
fat French fries, to serve

FOR THE TARTARE SAUCE:
1 cup prepared mayonnaise
¼ cup gherkins or pickling
  cucumbers, finely chopped
2 tbsp. freshly snipped chives
1 garlic clove, peeled and
  crushed
2–3 tbsp. capers, drained and
  chopped
pinch of cayenne pepper
corn oil for deep-frying

1 Mix together the bread crumbs, Parmesan cheese, seasoning, and oregano on a large plate. Lightly beat the egg in a shallow dish. Then, using a sharp knife, cut the flounder fillets into thick strips. Coat the flounder strips in the beaten egg, allowing any excess to drip back into the dish, then dip the strips into the bread crumbs until well coated. Place the goujons on a baking tray, cover and chill in the refrigerator for 30 minutes.

2 Meanwhile, to make the tartare sauce, mix together the mayonnaise, gherkins, chives, garlic, capers, and cayenne pepper. Stir, then season to taste with salt and pepper. Place in a bowl, cover loosely and store in the refrigerator until required.

3 Pour the oil into a large wok. Heat to 375° F (190° C) or until a small cube of bread turns golden and crisp in about 30 seconds. Cook the flounder goujons in batches for about 4 minutes, turning occasionally until golden. Using a slotted spoon, remove and drain on absorbent paper towels. Serve immediately with the tartare sauce and French fries.

TASTY TIP

For a change, try
replacing the white bread
in this recipe with flavored
focaccio or ciabatta.

EASTERN SPICY SCALLOPS

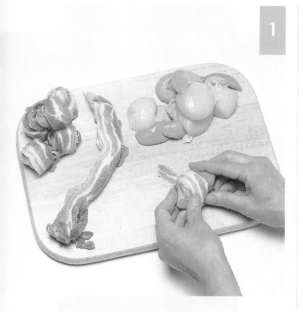

INGREDIENTS

Serves 6

12 fresh scallops, trimmed
12 slices bacon, rinded
2 tbsp. peanut oil
1 red onion, peeled and cut
  into wedges
1 red bell pepper, seeded and
  sliced
1 yellow bell pepper, seeded
  and sliced
2 garlic cloves, peeled and
  chopped
½ tsp. garam masala

1 tbsp. tomato paste
1 tbsp. paprika
4 tbsp. freshly chopped
  cilantro

TO SERVE:
freshly cooked noodles
Oriental-style salad

1 Remove the thin black thread from the scallops, rinse lightly and pat dry on absorbent paper towels. Wrap each scallop in a bacon slice. Place on a baking tray, cover and chill in the refrigerator for 30 minutes.

2 Meanwhile heat the wok, then add 1 tablespoon of the oil and stir-fry the onion for 3 minutes or until almost softened. Add the bell peppers and stir-fry for 5 minutes, stirring occasionally until browned. Transfer the vegetables to a plate and set aside.

3 Add the remaining oil to the wok, heat until almost smoking and then add the scallops, seam side down, and stir-fry for 2–3 minutes. Turn the scallops over and stir-fry for an additional 2–3 minutes until the bacon is crisp and the scallops are almost tender.

Add the garlic, garam masala, tomato paste, and paprika and stir until the scallops are coated.

4 Stir in the remaining ingredients with the reserved vegetables. Stir-fry for 1–2 minutes or until the vegetables are piping hot. Serve immediately with noodles and salad.

HELPFUL HINT

If you buy live scallops, to remove them from the shell, hold the flat part of the shell in your palm and slice a sharp knife between the shell halves, keeping the blade flat against the bottom shell. Slice through the meat, away from your hand, and open the shell. Cut the meat from the rounded shell. Remove the gray "frill" and wash well.

CRISPY SHRIMP STIR FRY

INGREDIENTS

Serves 4

3 tbsp. soy sauce

1 tsp. cornstarch

pinch of sugar

6 tbsp. peanut oil

1 lb. (450 g) raw shelled jumbo
shrimp, halved lengthwise

¾ cup carrots, peeled and cut
into matchsticks

1 in. (2.5 cm) piece fresh
ginger, peeled and cut into
matchsticks

1 cup snow peas, trimmed and
shredded

½ cup asparagus spears, cut
into short lengths

¾ cup beansprouts

¼ head Chinese cabbage or
bok choy, shredded

2 tsp. sesame oil

1 Mix together the soy sauce, cornstarch and sugar in a small bowl and set aside.

2 Heat a large wok, then add 3 tablespoons of the oil and heat until almost smoking. Add the shrimp and stir-fry for 4 minutes or until pink all over. Using a slotted spoon, transfer the shrimp to a plate and keep warm in a low oven.

3 Add the remaining oil to the wok and when just smoking, add the carrots and ginger and stir-fry for 1 minute or until slightly softened, then add the snow peas and stir-fry for an additional 1 minute. Add the asparagus and stir-fry for 4 minutes or until softened.

4 Add the beansprouts and Chinese cabbage and stir-fry for 2 minutes or until the cabbage is slightly wilted. Pour in the soy sauce mixture and return the shrimp to the wok. Stir-fry over a medium heat until piping hot, then add the sesame oil, give a final stir and serve immediately.

HELPFUL HINT

The long list of ingredients.
need not be daunting.
As always with wok cooking,
good preparation saves a lot
of time. It is essential to cut
everything into small,
uniform pieces and have
everything ready before
starting to cook.

SPICY COD RICE

INGREDIENTS   Serves 4

1 tbsp. all-purpose flour
1 tbsp. freshly chopped
   cilantro
1 tsp. ground cumin
1 tsp. ground coriander
1¼ lb. (550 g) thick cut cod
   fillet, skinned and cut into
   large chunks
4 tbsp. peanut oil
½ cup cashews
1 bunch scallions,
   trimmed and diagonally
   sliced

1 red chili, seeded and
   chopped
1 carrot, peeled and cut into
   matchsticks
1 cup frozen peas
5 cups cooked long-grain rice
2 tbsp. sweet chili sauce
2 tbsp. soy sauce

1 Mix together the flour, cilantro, cumin, and ground coriander on a large plate. Coat the cod in the spice mixture, then place on a baking tray, cover and chill in the refrigerator for 30 minutes.

2 Heat a large wok, then add 2 tablespoons of the oil and heat until almost smoking. Stir-fry the cashews for 1 minute until brown, then remove and set aside.

3 Add an additional 1 tablespoon of the oil and heat until almost smoking. Add the cod and stir-fry for 2 minutes. Using a spatula, turn the cod pieces over and cook for an additional 2 minutes until golden. Transfer to a warm plate, cover and keep warm.

4 Add the remaining oil to the wok, heat until almost smoking, then stir-fry the scallions and chili for 1 minute before adding the carrots and peas and stir-frying for an additional 2 minutes. Stir in the rice, chili sauce, soy sauce, and cashews and stir-fry for 3 more minutes. Add the cod, heat for 1 minute, then serve immediately.

HELPFUL HINT

Care is needed when frying nuts as they have a tendency to turn from golden to burned very quickly. An alternative is to toast them on a baking tray in the oven at 350° F (180° C) for about 5 minutes until they are golden and fragrant.

SOLE WITH RED WINE SAUCE

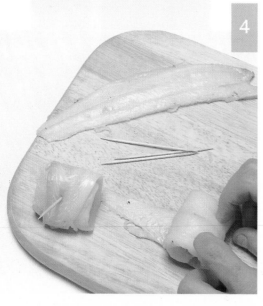

INGREDIENTS   Serves 4

4 tbsp. peanut oil
½ cup rindless bacon,
  diced
¾ cup shallots, peeled and
  chopped
2 cups button mushrooms,
  wiped
1 tbsp. all-purpose flour
2 tbsp. brandy
1¼ cups red wine
1 bouquet garni
1 garlic clove, peeled and
  chopped

salt and freshly ground black
  pepper
8 sole fillets, skinned and cut
  in half
sprigs of fresh parsley, to
  garnish

TO SERVE:
freshly cooked noodles
steamed snow peas

1 Heat a large wok, add the oil and heat. When almost smoking, stir-fry the bacon and shallots for 4–5 minutes or until golden. Using a slotted spoon, remove from the wok and keep warm. Add the mushrooms and stir-fry for 2 minutes, then remove and set aside.

2 Sprinkle the flour into the wok and carefully stir-fry over a medium heat for 30 seconds. Remove the wok from the heat, then return the bacon and shallots to the wok together with the brandy.

3 Stir in the red wine, bouquet garni, garlic, and season to taste with salt and pepper. Return to the heat and bring back to a boil, stirring until smooth, then simmer for about 5 minutes until the sauce is thickened.

4 Meanwhile roll the sole fillets up and secure with either kitchen string or toothpicks. Carefully add the rolled up sole fillets and reserved mushrooms with seasoning to the wok. Reduce the heat, cover with a lid or foil and simmer for an additional 8–10 minutes or until the fish is tender. Discard the bouquet garni, garnish with sprigs of fresh parsley and serve immediately with freshly cooked noodles and steamed snow peas.

HELPFUL HINT

Either lemon sole or
Dover sole may be used
in this recipe, depending
on the budget.

TROUT WITH CREAM SAUCE

INGREDIENTS   Serves 4

1¼ lb. (550 g) rainbow
  trout fillets, cut into
  pieces
salt and freshly ground
  black pepper
2 tbsp. all-purpose flour
1 tbsp. finely chopped dill
peanut oil for frying

FOR THE CREAM SAUCE:
½ stick butter
2 bunches scallions, trimmed
  and thickly sliced

1 garlic clove, peeled and
  finely chopped
1¼ cups dry white wine
½ cup heavy cream
3 tomatoes, peeled,
  seeded and cut
  into wedges
3 tbsp. freshly chopped basil
freshly snipped basil, to
  garnish
freshly cooked creamed herb
  potatoes, to serve

1 Remove as many of the tiny pin bones as possible from the trout fillets, rinse lightly and pat dry on absorbent paper towels. Season the flour and stir in the chopped dill, then use to coat the trout fillets.

2 Pour sufficient oil into a large wok to a depth of 1 inch (2.5 cm) deep. Heat until hot and cook the trout in batches for about 3–4 minutes, turning occasionally or until cooked. Using a slotted spoon, remove and drain on absorbent paper towels and keep warm. You may need to cook the trout in batches. Drain the wok and wipe clean.

3 Melt ¼ stick of the butter in the wok, then stir-fry the scallions and garlic for 2 minutes. Add the wine, bring to a boil and boil rapidly until reduced by half. Stir in the cream with the

tomatoes and basil, and bring to a boil. Simmer for 1 minute, then add seasoning to taste.

4 Add the trout to the sauce and heat through until piping hot. Garnish with freshly snipped basil and serve immediately on a bed of creamed herb potatoes.

HELPFUL HINT

Before cutting into pieces, lay the trout fillets on a clean chopping board and run your fingers from the tail end of the fish up to the head end. Use a pair of tweezers to remove any fine (pin) bones that you can feel.

CREAMY SPICY SHELLFISH

INGREDIENTS   Serves 4

2 tbsp. peanut oil

1 onion, peeled and chopped

1 in. (2.5 cm) piece fresh
   ginger, peeled and grated

½ lb. (225 g) bay scallops,
   cleaned and rinsed

1 garlic clove, peeled and
   chopped

2 tsp. ground cumin

1 tsp. paprika

1 tsp. coriander seeds,
   crushed

3 tbsp. lemon juice

2 tbsp. sherry

1¼ cups fish stock

½ cup heavy cream

2 cups shelled shrimp

2 cups cooked mussels,
   shelled

salt and freshly ground black
   pepper

2 tbsp. freshly chopped
   cilantro

1 Heat a large wok, then add the oil and, when hot, stir-fry the onion and ginger for 2 minutes or until softened. Add the scallops and stir-fry for 2 minutes or until the scallops are just cooked. Using a slotted spoon, carefully transfer the scallops to a bowl and keep warm in a low oven.

2 Stir in the garlic, ground cumin, paprika, and crushed coriander seeds and cook for 1 minute, stirring constantly. Pour in the lemon juice, sherry, and fish stock and bring to a boil. Boil rapidly until reduced by half and slightly thickened.

3 Stir in the heavy cream and return the scallops and any scallop juices to the wok. Bring to a boil and simmer for 1 minute. Add the shrimp and mussels and heat through until piping hot. Season to taste with

salt and pepper. Sprinkle with freshly chopped cilantro and serve immediately.

HELPFUL HINT

Bay scallops are difficult to find on the shell. They are usually bought frozen, therefore tend to have a lot of water in them. They should be drained well and pressed carefully between sheets of absorbent paper towels to remove the excess moisture, which will help to keep them from shrinking.

SQUID & SHRIMP WITH SAFFRON RICE

INGREDIENTS　　　　　　　　　Serves 4

2 tbsp. peanut oil

1 large onion, peeled and sliced

2 garlic cloves, peeled and chopped

1½ cups tomatoes, peeled, seeded and chopped

1 cup long-grain rice

¼ tsp. saffron strands

2½ cups fish stock

½ lb. (225 g) firm fish fillets, such as angler fish or cod

2 cups squid, cleaned

2 cups mussels with shells

¾ cup frozen or shelled fresh peas

2 cups shelled shrimp, thawed if frozen

salt and freshly ground black pepper

TO GARNISH:

8 whole cooked shrimp

lemon wedges

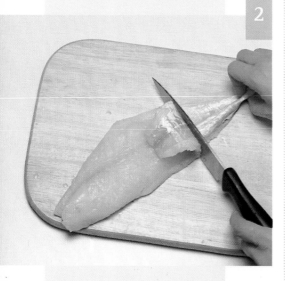

1 Heat a large wok, add the oil and, when hot, stir-fry the onion and garlic for 3 minutes. Add the tomatoes and continue to stir-fry for 1 minute before adding the rice, saffron, and stock. Bring to a boil, reduce the heat, cover and simmer for 10 minutes, stirring occasionally.

2 Meanwhile, remove any skin from the fish fillets, rinse lightly and cut into small cubes. Rinse the squid, pat dry with absorbent paper towels, then cut into rings and set aside. Scrub the mussels, discarding any that stay open after being tapped on the work surface. Cover with cold water and set aside until required.

3 Add the peas to the wok together with the fish and return to a gentle simmer. Cover and simmer for 5–10 minutes or until the rice is tender and most of the liquid has been absorbed.

4 Uncover and stir in the squid, the drained prepared mussels and the shelled shrimp. Recover and simmer for 5 minutes or until the mussels have opened. Discard any unopened ones. Season to taste with salt and pepper. Garnish with whole cooked shrimps and lemon wedges, then serve immediately.

HELPFUL HINT

Peel tomatoes by making a cross on the top of each one, cover with boiling water, then leave for 2 minutes. Drain and peel.

TEMPURA

INGREDIENTS
Serves 4

FOR THE BATTER:
1¾ cups all-purpose flour
pinch of baking soda
1 medium egg yolk

**FOR THE SHRIMP &
VEGETABLES:**
8–12 raw jumbo shrimp
1 carrot, peeled
1¾ cups button mushrooms,
wiped

1 green bell pepper, seeded
1 small eggplant, trimmed
1 onion, peeled
¾ cup fine green beans
½ cup sesame oil
1 cup vegetable oil for
deep-frying

TO SERVE:
soy sauce
chili dipping sauce

1 Sift the flour and baking soda into a mixing bowl. Blend 2 cups of water and the egg yolk together, then gradually beat into the flour mixture until a smooth batter is formed.

2 Shell the shrimp, leaving the tails intact, devein, then rinse lightly and pat dry with absorbent paper towels and set aside. Slice the carrot thinly then, using small pastry cutters, cut out fancy shapes. Cut the mushrooms in half, if large, and cut the bell pepper into chunks. Slice the eggplant, then cut into large chunks, together with the onion, and finally trim the fine green beans.

3 Pour the sesame oil and the vegetable oil into a large wok and heat to 350° F (180° C) or until a small spoonful of the batter dropped into the oil sizzles and cooks on impact.

4 Dip the shrimp and vegetables into the reserved batter (no more than 8 pieces at a time) and stir until lightly coated. Cook for 3 minutes, turning occasionally during cooking or until evenly golden. Using a slotted spoon, transfer the shrimp and vegetables onto absorbent paper towels and drain well. Keep warm. Repeat with the remaining ingredients. Serve immediately with soy sauce and chili dipping sauce.

FOOD FACT

The baking soda in the batter helps it to rise quickly when it hits the hot oil and then helps to keep the batter crispy once it is drained and served.

MEATBALLS WITH BEAN & TOMATO SAUCE

INGREDIENTS   Serves 4

1 large onion, peeled and finely chopped

1 red bell pepper, seeded and chopped

1 tbsp. freshly chopped oregano

½ tsp. hot paprika

15 oz. (425 g) can red kidney beans, drained

1⅓ cups fresh ground beef

salt and freshly ground black pepper

4 tbsp. corn oil

1 garlic clove, peeled and crushed

14 oz. (400 g) can chopped tomatoes

1 tbsp. freshly chopped cilantro, to garnish

freshly cooked rice, to serve

1 Make the meatballs by blending half the onion, half the red bell pepper, the oregano, the paprika, and 1½ cups of the red kidney beans in a blender or food processor for a few seconds. Add the beef with seasoning and blend until well mixed. Turn the mixture onto a lightly floured board and form into small balls.

2 Heat the wok, then add 2 tablespoons of the oil and, when hot, stir-fry the meatballs gently until well browned on all sides. Remove with a slotted spoon and keep warm.

3 Wipe the wok clean, then add the remaining oil and cook the remaining onion, pepper, and the garlic for 3–4 minutes until soft. Add the tomatoes, seasoning to taste, and remaining red kidney beans.

4 Return the meatballs to the wok, stir them into the sauce, then cover and simmer for 10 minutes. Sprinkle with the chopped cilantro and serve immediately with the freshly cooked rice.

FOOD FACT

Paprika gives this dish its distinctive flavor and color. Made from dried bell peppers, it is available hot or mild and even smoked. The best paprika comes from either Hungary or Spain, where in both places it is widely used.

CRISPY PORK WITH TANGY SAUCE

INGREDIENTS
Serves 4

¾ lb. (350 g) pork fillet
1 tbsp. light soy sauce
1 tbsp. dry sherry
salt and freshly ground black
   pepper
1 tbsp. sherry vinegar
1 tbsp. tomato paste
1 tbsp. dark soy sauce
2 tsp. golden brown sugar
⅔ cup chicken stock
1½ tsp. honey

8 tsp. cornstrach
1½ cups peanut oil
   for frying
1 medium egg

TO GARNISH:
fresh sprigs of dill
orange wedges

1 Remove and discard any fat and sinew from the pork fillet, then cut into ¾ inch (2 cm) cubes and place in a shallow dish. Blend the light soy sauce with the dry sherry and add seasoning. Pour over the pork and stir until the pork is lightly coated. Cover and allow to marinate in the refrigerator for at least 30 minutes, stirring occasionally.

2 Meanwhile blend the sherry vinegar, tomato paste, dark soy sauce, golden brown sugar, chicken stock, and honey together in a small saucepan and heat gently, stirring occasionally, until the sugar has dissolved. Then bring to a boil.

3 Blend 2 teaspoons of cornstarch with 1 tablespoon of water and stir into the sauce. Cook, stirring until smooth and thickened, and either keep warm or reheat when required.

4 Heat the oil in the wok to 375° F (190° C). Beat together the remaining 6 teaspoons of cornstarch and the egg to make a smooth batter. Drain the pork if necessary, then dip the pieces into the batter, allowing any excess to drip back into the bowl. Cook in the hot oil for 2–3 minutes or until golden and tender. Drain on paper towels. Cook the pork in batches until it is all cooked, then garnish and serve immediately with the sauce.

HELPFUL HINT

Mix cornstarch with a little of the hot, not boiling, sauce or blend to a paste with a little cold liquid. Stir into the hot liquor and cook stirring to thicken.

BEEF FAJITAS WITH AVOCADO SAUCE

INGREDIENTS   Serves 3–6

2 tbsp. corn oil

1 lb. (450 g) rump steak, trimmed and cut into strips

2 garlic cloves, peeled and crushed

1 tsp. ground cumin

¼ tsp. cayenne pepper

1 tbsp. paprika

8 oz. (225 g) can chopped tomatoes

7 oz. (200 g) can red kidney beans, drained

1 tbsp. freshly chopped cilantro

1 avocado, peeled, pitted, and chopped

1 shallot, peeled and chopped

1 large tomato, peeled, seeded and chopped

1 red chili, diced

1 tbsp. lemon juice

6 large flour tortilla pancakes

3–4 tbsp. sour cream

green salad, to serve

1 Heat the wok, add the oil, then stir-fry the beef for 3–4 minutes. Add the garlic and spices and cook for an additional 2 minutes. Stir the tomatoes into the wok, bring to a boil, cover and simmer gently for 5 minutes.

2 Meanwhile blend the kidney beans in a food processor until slightly broken up, then add to the wok. Continue to cook for an additional 5 minutes, adding 2–3 tablespoons of water. The mixture should be thick and fairly dry. Stir in the chopped cilantro.

3 Mix the chopped avocado, shallot, tomato, chili, and lemon juice together. Spoon into a serving dish and set aside.

4 When ready to serve, warm the flour tortillas and spread

with a little sour cream. Place a spoonful of the beef mixture on top, followed by a spoonful of the avocado sauce, then roll up. Repeat until all the mixture is used up. Serve immediately with a green salad.

HELPFUL HINT

The avocado sauce should not be made too far in advance, as avocado has a tendency to discolor. If it is necessary to make it some time ahead, the surface of the sauce should be covered with plastic wrap.

CARIBBEAN PORK

INGREDIENTS　　　　　　　　Serves 4

1 lb. (450 g) pork fillet
1 in. (2.5 cm) piece fresh
　ginger, peeled and grated
½ tsp. crushed dried chilies
2 garlic cloves, peeled and
　crushed
2 tbsp. freshly chopped
　parsley
⅔ cup orange juice
2 tbsp. dark soy sauce

2 tbsp. peanut oil
1 large onion, peeled and
　sliced into wedges
1 large zucchini, trimmed and
　cut into strips
1 orange bell pepper, seeded
　and cut into strips
1 ripe but firm mango, peeled
　and pitted
freshly cooked rice, to serve

1 Cut the pork fillet into thin strips and place in a shallow dish. Sprinkle with the ginger, chilies, garlic, and 1 tablespoon of the parsley. Blend together the orange juice, soy sauce, and 1 tablespoon of the oil, then pour over the pork. Cover and chill in the refrigerator for 30 minutes, stirring occasionally. Remove the pork strips with a slotted spoon and set the marinade aside.

2 Heat the wok, pour in the remaining oil and stir-fry the pork for 3–4 minutes. Add the onion rings, the zucchini and orange bell pepper strips and cook for 2 minutes. Add the reserved marinade to the wok and stir-fry for an additional 2 minutes.

3 Remove the pit from the mango, cut the flesh into strips, then stir it into the pork mixture. Continue to stir-fry until everything is piping hot. Garnish with the remaining parsley and serve immediately with plenty of freshly cooked rice.

HELPFUL HINT

Pork fillet, or tenderloin, as it is sometimes known, is a very tender cut and is always boneless. It may have some sinew attached and this should be removed with a sharp knife.

SAUSAGE & BACON RISOTTO

INGREDIENTS   Serves 4

1 cup long-grain rice
1 tbsp. olive oil
¼ stick butter
4 cocktail or small link
  sausages,
1 shallot, peeled and finely
  chopped
⅓ cup thick slices of bacon,
  chopped
1¼ cups chorizo or similar
  spicy sausage, cut into chunks

1 green bell pepper, seeded
  and cut into strips
7 oz. (200 g) can corn, drained
2 tbsp. freshly chopped
  parsley
½ cup mozzarella cheese,
  shredded

1 Cook the rice in a saucepan of boiling salted water for 15 minutes or until tender or according to the package directions. Drain and rinse in cold water. Drain again and leave until completely cold.

2 Meanwhile heat the wok, pour in the oil and melt the butter. Cook the cocktail sausages, turning continuously until cooked. Remove with a slotted spoon, cut in half and keep warm.

3 Add the shallot and bacon to the wok and cook for 2–3 minutes until cooked but not browned. Add the spicy sausage and green bell pepper and stir-fry for an additional 3 minutes.

4 Add the cold rice and the corn to the wok and stir-fry for 2 minutes, then return the cooked sausages to the wok and

stir over the heat until everything is piping hot. Garnish with the freshly chopped parsley and serve immediately with a little shredded mozzarella cheese.

HELPFUL HINT

It is now possible to buy packages of thick bacon slices but if these are unavailable, try to get bacon in a piece from a delicatessen. Cut the bacon into ½ inch (1 cm) slices, then cut the slices crosswise into ½ inch (1 cm) pieces.

SPEEDY PORK WITH YELLOW BEAN SAUCE

INGREDIENTS
Serves 4

1 lb. (450 g) pork fillet
2 tbsp. light soy sauce
2 tbsp. orange juice
2 tsp. cornstarch
3 tbsp. peanut oil
2 garlic cloves, peeled and
   crushed
1 cup carrots, peeled and cut
   into matchsticks
¾ cup fine green beans,
   trimmed and halved

2 scallions, trimmed and cut
   into strips
4 tbsp. yellow bean sauce
1 tbsp. freshly chopped Italian
   parsley, to garnish
freshly cooked egg noodles,
   to serve

1 Remove any fat or sinew from the pork fillet, and cut into thin strips. Blend the soy sauce, orange juice, and cornstarch in a bowl and mix thoroughly. Place the meat in a shallow dish, pour over the soy sauce mixture, cover and allow to marinate in the refrigerator for 1 hour. Drain with a slotted spoon, setting the marinade aside.

2 Heat the wok, then add 2 tablespoons of the oil and stir-fry the pork with the garlic for 2 minutes or until the meat is sealed. Remove with a slotted spoon and set aside.

3 Add the remaining oil to the wok and cook the carrots, beans, and scallions for about 3 minutes until tender but still crisp. Return the pork to the wok with the reserved marinade, then pour over the yellow bean sauce. Stir-fry for an additional 1–2 minutes or until the pork is tender. Sprinkle with the chopped parsley and serve immediately with freshly cooked egg noodles.

FOOD FACT

Yellow bean sauce is available from large supermarkets or Asian grocery stores. It is one of many readymade sauces commonly used in Chinese cookery. Black bean sauce may be substituted.

LAMB WITH BLACK CHERRY SAUCE

INGREDIENTS   Serves 4

1¼ lb. (550 g) lamb fillet
2 tbsp. light soy sauce
1 tsp. Chinese five spice powder
¼ cup fresh orange juice
½ cup black cherry jelly
⅔ cup red wine
⅓ cup fresh black cherries

1 tbsp. peanut oil
1 tbsp. freshly chopped
  cilantro, to garnish

TO SERVE:
thawed frozen peas
freshly cooked noodles

1 Remove the skin and any fat from the lamb fillet and cut into thin slices. Place in a shallow dish. Mix together the soy sauce, Chinese five spice powder, and orange juice and pour over the meat. Cover and leave in the refrigerator for at least 30 minutes.

2 Meanwhile blend the jelly and the wine together, pour into a small saucepan and bring to a boil. Simmer gently for 10 minutes until slightly thickened. Carefully remove the pits from the cherries and if possible try to keep them whole.

3 Drain the lamb when ready to cook. Heat the wok, add the oil and, when the oil is hot, stir-fry the slices of lamb for 3–5 minutes or until just slightly pink inside or cooked to personal preference.

4 Spoon the lamb into a warm serving dish and serve immediately with a little of the cherry sauce drizzled over.

Garnish with the chopped cilantro and the whole cherries and serve immediately with peas, freshly cooked noodles, and the remaining sauce.

TASTY TIP

Fresh cherries have a very short season in early summer, so if you want to make this dish at other times, substitute canned cherries in juice. Drain the cherries well before adding to the sauce.

HONEY PORK WITH RICE NOODLES & CASHEWS

INGREDIENTS   Serves 4

1⅔ cups rice noodles
1 lb. (450 g) pork fillet
2 tbsp. peanut oil
1 tbsp. softened butter
1 onion, peeled and finely
  sliced into rings
2 garlic cloves, peeled and
  crushed
1 cup baby button
  mushrooms, halved
3 tbsp. light soy sauce

3 tbsp. honey
½ cup unsalted cashews
1 red chili, seeded and finely
  chopped
4 scallions, trimmed
  and finely chopped
freshly stir-fried vegetables,
  to serve

1 Soak the rice noodles in boiling water for 4 minutes or according to the package directions. Drain and set aside.

2 Trim and slice the pork fillet into thin strips. Heat the wok, pour in the oil and butter, and stir-fry the pork for 4–5 minutes until cooked. Remove with a slotted spoon and keep warm.

3 Add the onion to the wok and stir-fry for 2 minutes. Stir in the garlic and mushrooms and cook for an additional 2 minutes or until juices start to run from the mushrooms.

4 Blend the soy sauce with the honey, then return the pork to the wok with this mixture. Add the cashews and cook for 1–2 minutes, then add the rice noodles a little at a time. Stir-fry

until everything is piping hot. Sprinkle with chopped chili and scallions. Serve immediately with freshly stir-fried vegetables.

TASTY TIP

Heat a wok until really hot, then add 1 tablespoon of oil. Swirl around the wok, then add 1 chopped garlic clove and a little grated ginger. Add a finely sliced red, green, and yellow bell pepper, some snow peas and scallion. Stir-fry for 3–4 minutes, then serve with the pork.

SWEET-&-SOUR PORK

INGREDIENTS   Serves 4

1 lb. (450 g) pork fillet
1 medium egg white
4 tsp. cornstarch
salt and freshly ground black
   pepper
1 cup peanut oil
1 small onion, peeled and
   finely sliced
⅔ cup carrots, peeled and cut
   into matchsticks

1 in. (2.5 cm) piece ginger,
   peeled and cut into strips
⅔ cup orange juice
⅔ cup chicken stock
1 tbsp. light soy sauce
7 oz. (200 g) can pineapple
   pieces, drained with juice set
   aside
1 tbsp. white wine vinegar
1 tbsp. freshly chopped parsley
freshly cooked rice, to serve

1 Trim, then cut the pork fillet into small cubes. In a bowl, beat the egg white and cornstarch with a little seasoning, then add the pork to the egg white mixture and stir until the cubes are well coated.

2 Heat the wok, then add the oil. Heat until very hot before adding the pork and stir-frying for 30 seconds. Turn off the heat and continue to stir for 3 minutes. The meat should be white and sealed. Drain off the oil, set the pork aside and wipe the wok clean.

3 Pour 2 teaspoons of the drained peanut oil back into the wok and cook the onion, carrots, and ginger for 2–3 minutes. Blend the orange juice with the chicken stock, and soy sauce and make up to 1¼ cups with the reserved pineapple juice.

4 Return the pork to the wok with the juice mixture and simmer for 3–4 minutes. Then stir in the pineapple pieces and vinegar. Heat through, then sprinkle with the chopped parsley and serve immediately with freshly cooked rice.

TASTY TIP

If preferred, the pineapple pieces can be replaced with 1 large orange that has been peeled, segmented, and coarsely chopped.

CHILI LAMB

INGREDIENTS
Serves 4

1¼ lb. (550 g) lamb fillet
3 tbsp. peanut oil
1 large onion, peeled and
   finely sliced
2 garlic cloves, peeled and
   crushed
4 tsp. cornstarch
4 tbsp. hot chili sauce
2 tbsp. white wine vinegar
4 tsp. dark brown sugar
1 tsp. Chinese five spice powder

sprigs of fresh cilantro, to
garnish

TO SERVE:
freshly cooked noodles
4 tbsp. plain yogurt

1 Trim the lamb fillet, discarding any fat or sinew, then place it on a clean chopping board and cut into thin strips. Heat a wok and pour in 2 tablespoons of the peanut oil and, when hot, stir-fry the lamb for 3–4 minutes or until it is browned. Remove the lamb strips with their juices and set aside.

2 Add the remaining oil to the wok, then stir-fry the onion and garlic for 2 minutes or until softened. Remove with a slotted spoon and add to the lamb.

3 Blend the cornstarch with ½ cup of cold water, then stir in the chili sauce, vinegar, sugar, and Chinese five spice powder. Pour this into the wok, increase the heat and bring the mixture to a boil. Cook for 30 seconds or until the sauce thickens.

4 Return the lamb to the wok with the onion and garlic, stir thoroughly and heat through until piping hot. Garnish with sprigs of fresh cilantro and serve immediately with freshly cooked noodles, topped with a spoonful of plain yogurt.

TASTY TIP

It is important to use canned hot chili sauce rather than Tabasco in this recipe. Chili sauce is less fiery, though still quite hot, so taste a tiny bit first, then adjust the quantity according to taste.

SPICY LAMB IN YOGURT SAUCE

INGREDIENTS   Serves 4

1 tsp. hot chili powder
1 tsp. ground cinnamon
1 tsp. medium hot curry
  powder
1 tsp. ground cumin
salt and freshly ground black
  pepper
2 tbsp. peanut oil
1 lb. (450 g) lamb fillet, trimmed
4 cardamom pods, bruised
4 whole cloves
1 onion, peeled and finely
  sliced
2 garlic cloves, peeled and
  crushed

1 in. (2.5 cm) piece fresh
  ginger, peeled and grated
⅔ cup plain yogurt
1 tbsp. freshly chopped
  cilantro
2 scallions, trimmed and finely
  sliced

TO SERVE:

freshly cooked rice
naan or Indian-style bread

1 Blend the chili powder, cinnamon, curry powder, cumin, and seasoning with 2 tablespoons of the oil in a bowl and set aside. Cut the lamb fillet into thin strips, add to the spice and oil mixture and stir until coated thoroughly. Cover and allow to marinate in the refrigerator for at least 30 minutes.

2 Heat the wok, then pour in the remaining oil. When hot, add the cardamom pods and cloves and stir-fry for 10 seconds. Add the onion, garlic, and ginger to the wok and stir-fry for 3–4 minutes until softened.

3 Add the lamb with the marinading ingredients and stir-fry for an additional 3 minutes until cooked. Pour in the yogurt, stir thoroughly and heat until piping hot. Sprinkle with the chopped cilantro and sliced scallions, then serve immediately with freshly cooked rice and naan bread.

HELPFUL HINT

Whole spices retain their freshness far longer than ready ground ones. It is therefore preferable to buy whole spices in small quantities and grind them in a clean coffee grinder or spice grinder as they are needed.

PORK IN PEANUT SAUCE

INGREDIENTS
Serves 4

1 lb. (450 g) pork fillet
2 tbsp. light soy sauce
1 tbsp. vinegar
1 tsp. sugar
1 tsp. Chinese five spice
  powder
2–4 garlic cloves, peeled
  and crushed
2 tbsp. peanut oil
1 large onion, peeled and
  finely sliced
⅔ cup carrots, peeled and cut
  into matchsticks

2 celery stalks, trimmed and
  sliced
¾ cup fine green beans,
  trimmed and halved
3 tbsp. smooth peanut butter
1 tbsp. freshly chopped Italian
  parsley

TO SERVE:
freshly cooked basmati and
  wild rice
green salad

1 Remove any fat or sinew from the pork fillet, cut into thin strips and set aside. Blend the soy sauce, vinegar, sugar, Chinese five spice powder, and garlic in a bowl and add the pork. Cover and allow to marinate in the refrigerator for at least 30 minutes.

2 Drain the pork, setting aside any marinade. Heat the wok, then add the oil and, when hot, stir-fry the pork for 3–4 minutes or until sealed.

3 Add the onion, carrots, celery, and beans to the wok and stir-fry for 4–5 minutes or until the meat is tender and the vegetables are softened.

4 Blend the reserved marinade, the peanut butter, and 2 tablespoons of hot water together. When smooth, stir into the wok and cook for several minutes more until the sauce is thick and the pork is piping hot. Sprinkle with the chopped parsley and serve immediately with the basmati and wild rice and a green salad.

TASTY TIP

For a really tasty appetizer idea, allow the pork strips in the peanut sauce to cool slightly, then serve wrapped in small, crisp lettuce leaves.

STIR-FRIED BEEF WITH VERMOUTH

INGREDIENTS   Serves 4

¾ lb. (350 g) beef steak, such as rump or sirloin

2 tbsp. all-purpose flour

salt and freshly ground black pepper

3 tbsp. corn oil

2 shallots, peeled and finely chopped

1 cup button mushrooms, wiped and halved

2 tbsp. freshly chopped tarragon

3 tbsp. dry vermouth or Martini

⅔ cup light cream

1⅔ cups stir-fry noodles

2 tsp. sesame oil

1 Trim the beef and cut into thin strips. Place the flour in a bowl and add salt and pepper to taste, then stir well. Add the beef and stir until well coated, then remove from the flour and set aside.

2 Heat a wok, then add the oil and, when hot, add the shallots and stir-fry for 2 minutes. Add the beef strips and stir-fry for 3–4 minutes before adding the mushrooms and 1 tablespoon of the chopped tarragon. Stir-fry for an additional 1 minute.

3 Pour in the vermouth or Martini, stirring continuously, then add the cream. Cook for 2–3 minutes or until the sauce is slightly thickened and the meat is cooked thoroughly. Adjust the seasoning and keep warm.

4 Meanwhile place the noodles in a large saucepan and cover with boiling water. Let stand for

4 minutes, then drain thoroughly and return to the wok. Add the sesame oil to the noodles and stir-fry for 1–2 minutes or until heated through thoroughly. Pile the noodles onto serving dishes, top with the beef and serve immediately.

FOOD FACT

Vermouth is made using wormwood. The word "vermouth" may, in fact, be a French corruption of "wormwood." Wormwood is also used in the production of absinthe.

PORK WITH SPRING VEGETABLES & SWEET CHILI SAUCE

INGREDIENTS   Serves 4

1 lb. (450 g) pork fillet

2 tbsp. corn oil

2 garlic cloves, peeled and
  crushed

1 in. (2.5 cm) piece fresh
  ginger, peeled and grated

⅔ cup carrots, peeled and cut
  into matchsticks

4 scallions, trimmed

1 cup snow peas

1 cup baby corn

2 tbsp. sweet chili sauce

2 tbsp. light soy sauce

1 tbsp. vinegar

½ tsp. sugar, or to taste

¾ cup beansprouts

1 tbsp. grated orange zest

freshly cooked rice, to serve

1 Trim, then cut the pork fillet into thin strips and set aside. Heat a wok and pour in the oil. When hot, add the garlic and ginger and stir-fry for 30 seconds. Add the carrots to the wok and continue to stir-fry for about 1–2 minutes or until they start to soften.

2 Slice the scallions lengthwise, then cut into three lengths. Trim the snow peas and the baby corn. Add the scalllions, snow peas, and corn to the wok and stir-fry for 30 seconds.

3 Add the pork to the wok and continue to stir-fry for 2–3 minutes or until the meat is sealed and browned all over. Blend the sweet chili sauce, soy sauce, vinegar, and sugar together, then stir into the wok with the beansprouts.

4 Continue to stir-fry until the meat is cooked and the vegetables are tender but still crisp. Sprinkle with the orange zest and serve immediately with the freshly cooked rice.

TASTY TIP

It is tempting to assume that sweet chili sauce is not hot but it can still have a good chili kick. It is wise to taste a little before adding it to the sauce and adjust the quantity according to taste.

BEEF WITH PAPRIKA

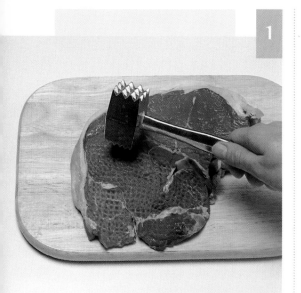

INGREDIENTS

Serves 4

1½ lb. (700 g) rump steak
3 tbsp. all-purpose flour
salt and freshly ground
   black pepper
1 tbsp. paprika
1½ cups long-grain
   rice
¾ stick butter
1 tsp. oil
1 onion, peeled and thinly
   sliced into rings

2 cups button mushrooms,
   wiped and sliced
2 tsp. dry sherry
⅔ cup sour cream
2 tbsp. freshly snipped chives
bundle of chives, to garnish

1 Beat the steak until very thin, then trim off and discard the fat and cut into thin strips. Season the flour with the salt, pepper, and paprika, then toss the steak in the flour until coated.

2 Meanwhile place the rice in a saucepan of boiling salted water and simmer for 15 minutes until tender or according to the package directions. Drain the rice, then return to the saucepan, add ¼ stick of the butter, cover and keep warm.

3 Heat the wok, then add the oil and ¼ stick of the butter. When hot, stir-fry the meat for 3–5 minutes until sealed. Remove from the wok with a slotted spoon and set aside. Add the remaining butter to the wok and stir-fry the onion rings and button mushrooms for 3–4 minutes.

4 Add the sherry while the wok is very hot, then turn down the heat. Return the steak to the wok with the sour cream and seasoning to taste. Heat through until piping hot, then sprinkle with the snipped chives. Garnish with bundles of chives and serve immediately with the cooked rice.

TASTY TIP

The button mushrooms in this recipe could be replaced by exotic or wild mushrooms. Chanterelles go particularly well with beef, as do ceps.

FRIED RICE WITH CHILI BEEF

INGREDIENTS   Serves 4

½ lb. (225 g) beef fillet
1½ cups long-grain rice
4 tbsp. peanut oil
3 onions, peeled and thinly
   sliced
2 hot red chilies, seeded and
   finely chopped
2 tbsp. light soy sauce
2 tsp. tomato paste
salt and freshly ground black
   pepper

2 tbsp. milk
2 tbsp. flour
1 tbsp. butter
2 medium eggs

1 Trim the beef fillet, discarding any fat, then cut into thin strips and set aside. Cook the rice in salted boiling water for 15 minutes or according to the package directions. Drain and set aside.

2 Heat a wok and add 3 tablespoons of oil. When hot, add 2 of the sliced onions and stir-fry for 2–3 minutes. Add the beef to the wok, with the chilies and stir-fry for an additional 3 minutes or until tender.

3 Add the rice to the wok with the soy sauce and tomato paste. Stir-fry for 1–2 minutes or until piping hot. Season to taste with salt and pepper and keep warm. Meanwhile toss the remaining onion in the milk, then the flour in batches. In a small skillet sauté the onion in the last 1 tablespoon of oil until crisp, then set aside.

4 Melt the butter in a small omelet pan. Beat the eggs with 2 teaspoons of water and pour into the pan. Cook gently, stirring frequently until the egg has set, forming an omelet, then slide onto a clean chopping board and cut into thin strips. Add to the fried rice, sprinkle with the crispy onion and serve immediately.

HELPFUL HINT

To determine how hot a chili is, the rule of thumb is "the smaller the chili, the hotter it is." Small Thai bird's eye chilies are extremely hot and should be used very sparingly.

LAMB'S LIVER WITH BACON & ONIONS

INGREDIENTS

Serves 4

¾ lb. (350 g) lamb's liver
2 heaped tbsp. all-purpose
  flour
salt and freshly ground
  black pepper
2 tbsp. peanut oil
2 large onions, peeled and
  finely sliced
2 garlic cloves, peeled and
  chopped
1 red chili, seeded and
  chopped

¾ cup bacon
¼ stick butter, plus 1 tbsp.
1¼ cups lamb or beef stock
2 tbsp. freshly chopped
  parsley

TO SERVE:
freshly cooked creamy
  mashed potatoes
freshly cooked green
  vegetables
freshly cooked carrots

1 Trim the liver, discarding any sinew or tubes, and thinly slice. Season the flour with salt and pepper, then use to coat the liver. Set aside

2 Heat a wok, then add the oil and, when hot, add the sliced onion, garlic, and chili and cook for 5–6 minutes or until soft and browned. Remove from the wok with a slotted spoon and set aside. Cut each slice of the bacon in half and stir-fry for 3–4 minutes or until cooked. Remove with a slotted spoon and add to the onions.

3 Melt the butter in the wok and cook the liver on all sides until browned and crisp. Pour in the stock and allow to bubble fiercely for 1–2 minutes. Return the onions and bacon to the wok, stir thoroughly, then cover. Simmer gently for 10 minutes or until the liver is tender. Sprinkle with the parsley and serve immediately with mashed potatoes, green vegetables, and carrots.

TASTY TIP

For creamy mashed potatoes, peel and cube 3 medium floury potatoes. Cover with cold water and add salt. Bring to a boil and simmer for 15–20 minutes until tender. Drain well and return to the heat for a few seconds to dry out. Add ½ stick of butter and 4 tablespoons of whole milk and season. Mash thoroughly, adding a little more milk if necessary until smooth and creamy.

SHREDDED BEEF IN HOISIN SAUCE

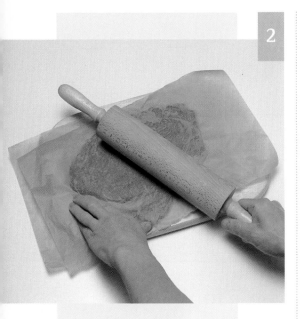

INGREDIENTS   Serves 4

2 celery stalks	2 tbsp. light soy sauce
3 medium carrots	1 tbsp. hoisin sauce
1 lb. (450 g) rump steak	1 tbsp. sweet chili sauce
2 tbsp. cornstarch	2 tbsp. dry sherry
salt and freshly ground	9 oz. (250 g) package fine egg
black pepper	thread noodles
2 tbsp. corn oil	1 tbsp. freshly chopped
4 scallions, trimmed	cilantro
and chopped	

1 Trim the celery and peel the carrots, then cut into fine matchsticks and set aside.

2 Place the steak between 2 sheets of waxed paper or parchment paper. Beat the steak with a meat mallet or rolling pin until very thin, then slice into strips. Season the cornstarch with salt and pepper and use to coat the steak. Set aside.

3 Heat a wok, add the oil and, when hot, add the scallions and cook for 1 minute, then add the steak and stir-fry for an additional 3–4 minutes or until the meat is sealed.

4 Add the celery and carrot matchsticks to the wok and stir-fry for an additional 2 minutes before adding the soy, hoisin and chlli sauces, and the sherry. Bring to a boil and simmer for 2–3 minutes or until the steak is tender and the vegetables are cooked.

5 Plunge the fine egg noodles into boiling water and leave for 4 minutes. Drain, then spoon onto a large serving dish. Top with the cooked shredded steak, then sprinkle with chopped cilantro and serve immediately.

TASTY TIP

Although this recipe calls for dry sherry, Chinese rice wine may be substituted if you can find it.

PORK WITH ASSORTED PEPPERS

INGREDIENTS   Serves 4

1 lb. (450 g) pork fillet
2 tbsp. peanut oil
1 onion, peeled and thinly
   sliced
1 red bell pepper, seeded and
   cut into strips
1 yellow bell pepper, seeded
   and cut into strips
1 orange bell pepper, seeded
   and cut into strips
2 garlic cloves, peeled and
   crushed

2 tsp. paprika
14 oz. (400 g) can chopped
   tomatoes
1¼ cups pork or chicken stock
1 tsp. dark brown sugar
salt and freshly ground black
   pepper
handful fresh oregano leaves
4½ cups penne or pasta twists
2 tbsp. shredded mozzarella
   cheese

1 Trim the pork fillet, discarding any sinew and fat, then cut into small cubes. Heat the wok, add the oil and, when hot, stir-fry the pork for 3–4 minutes until they are brown and sealed. Remove the pork from the wok and set aside.

2 Add the sliced onions to the wok and stir-fry until they are softened but not browned, then add the bell pepper strips and stir-fry for an additional 3–4 minutes.

3 Stir in the garlic, paprika, chopped tomatoes, stock, sugar, and seasoning and bring to a boil. Simmer, uncovered, stirring occasionally for 15 minutes or until the sauce has reduced and thickened. Return the pork to the wok and simmer for an additional 5–10 minutes. Sprinkle with the oregano leaves.

4 Cook the pasta for 3–4 minutes until "al dente" or according to the package directions, then drain and serve immediately with the pork and shredded mozzarella cheese.

TASTY TIP

Fresh oregano has a fairly
powerful flavor, very similar
to that of marjoram.
1 teaspoon of dried oregano
may be used if preferred.

Beef Curry with Lemon & Risotto Rice

INGREDIENTS   Serves 4

1 lb. (450 g) beef fillet
1 tbsp. olive oil
2 tbsp. green curry paste
1 green bell pepper, seeded
  and cut into strips
1 red bell pepper, seeded
  and cut into strips
1 celery stalk, trimmed and
  sliced
2 tbsp. lemon juice
2 tsp. Thai fish sauce

2 tsp. raw sugar
1 cup risotto rice
1 tbsp. butter
2 tbsp. freshly chopped
  cilantro
4 tbsp. sour cream

1 Trim the beef fillet, discarding any fat, then cut across the grain into thin slices. Heat a wok, add the oil and, when hot, add the green curry paste and cook for 30 seconds. Add the beef strips and stir-fry for 3–4 minutes.

2 Add the sliced bell peppers and the celery and continue to stir-fry for 2 minutes. Add the lemon juice, Thai fish sauce, and sugar and cook for an additional 3–4 minutes or until the beef is tender and cooked to personal preference.

3 Meanwhile cook the risotto rice in a saucepan of lightly salted boiling water for 15–20 minutes or until tender. Drain, rinse with boiling water and drain again. Return to the saucepan and add the butter. Cover and allow

the butter to melt before turning it out onto a large serving dish. Sprinkle the cooked curry with the chopped cilantro and serve immediately with the rice and sour cream.

TASTY TIP

Fresh green curry paste can be made at home. Using a blender or spice grinder, finely chop together 3–4 seeded hot green chilies, 1 lemon grass stalk, 2 shallots, 3 garlic cloves, 1 inch (2.5 cm) piece galangal or ginger, 1 teaspoon ground coriander, ½ teaspoon ground cumin, 2 kaffir lime leaves, and a handful of fresh cilantro. Keep in the refrigerator.

LEMON CHICKEN

INGREDIENTS   Serves 4

1 lb. (450 g) skinless, boneless
  chicken breast fillets, cubed
1 medium egg white, beaten
1 tsp. salt
1 tbsp. sesame oil
1 tbsp. cornstarch
1 cup peanut oil
6 tbsp. chicken stock
1 tbsp. grated lemon zest
2 tbsp. lemon juice
1 tbsp. sugar

1 tbsp. light soy sauce
2 tbsp. Chinese rice wine or
  dry sherry
3 large garlic cloves, peeled
  and finely chopped
1–2 tsp. dried red chilies,
  crushed
shredded fresh red chllies, to
  garnish
freshly steamed white rice, to
  serve

1 Place the cubes of chicken in a large bowl then add the beaten egg white, salt, 1 teaspoon of sesame oil, and 1 teaspoon of cornstarch. Mix lightly together until all the chicken is coated, then chill in the refrigerator for 20 minutes.

2 Heat the wok until very hot and add the oil. When hot, remove the wok from the heat and add the chicken. Stir-fry for 2 minutes or until the chicken turns white, then remove with a slotted spoon and drain on absorbent paper towels.

3 Wipe the wok clean and heat until hot again. Add the stock, lemon zest, lemon juice, sugar, soy sauce, Chinese rice wine, garlic, and crushed chilies and bring to a boil. Blend the remaining cornstarch to a smooth paste with 1 tablespoon of water and add to the wok. Stir, then

simmer for 1 minute. Add the chicken cubes and stir-fry for 2–3 minutes. Add the remaining sesame oil, garnish with shredded chilies and serve immediately with freshly steamed rice.

HELPFUL HINT

If possible, use unwaxed lemons for this dish and for any dish using lemon zest. If these are unavailable, pour hot water over the lemons, then scrub them to remove the wax.

CHICKEN IN BLACK BEAN SAUCE

INGREDIENTS   Serves 4

1 lb. (450 g) skinless, boneless chicken breast fillets, cut into strips
1 tbsp. light soy sauce
2 tbsp. Chinese rice wine or dry sherry
salt
1 tsp. sugar
1 tsp. sesame oil
2 tsp. cornstarch
2 tbsp. corn oil
2 green bell peppers, seeded and diced
1 tbsp. freshly grated ginger

2 garlic cloves, peeled and coarsely chopped
2 shallots, peeled and finely chopped
4 scallions, trimmed and finely sliced
3 tbsp. salted black beans, chopped
⅔ cup chicken stock
shredded scallions, to garnish
freshly cooked egg noodles, to serve

1 Place the chicken strips in a large bowl. Mix together the soy sauce, Chinese rice wine or sherry, a little salt, sugar, sesame oil, and cornstarch and pour over the chicken.

2 Heat the wok over a high heat, add the oil and, when very hot, add the chicken strips and stir-fry for 2 minutes. Add the green bell peppers and stir-fry for an additional 2 minutes. Then add the ginger, garlic, shallots, scallions, and black beans and continue to stir-fry for another 2 minutes.

3 Add 4 tablespoons of the stock, stir-fry for 1 minute, then pour in the remaining stock and bring to a boil. Reduce the heat and simmer the sauce for 3–4 minutes or until the

chicken is cooked and the sauce has thickened slightly. Garnish with the shredded scallions and serve immediately with noodles.

FOOD FACT

Black beans, also known as salted black beans, are soy beans that have been preserved by being fermented with salt and spices. They have a distinctive salty taste, a rich savory aroma and are often used as a seasoning in conjunction with garlic or ginger. Buy the beans either in cans, in which case they will need rinsing and draining, or dry in bags. Dried black beans will keep indefinitely in an airtight container.

GREEN CHICKEN CURRY

INGREDIENTS   Serves 4

1 onion, peeled and chopped

3 lemon grass stalks, outer leaves discarded and finely sliced

2 garlic cloves, peeled and finely chopped

1 tbsp. freshly grated ginger

3 green chilies

2 tsp. grated lime zest

1 tbsp. lime juice

2 tbsp. peanut oil

2 tbsp. Thai fish sauce

6 tbsp. freshly chopped cilantro

6 tbsp. freshly chopped basil

1 lb. (450 g) skinless, boneless chicken breasts, cut into strips

¾ cup fine green beans, trimmed

2 cups coconut milk

fresh basil leaves, to garnish

freshly cooked rice, to serve

1 Place the onion, lemon grass, garlic, ginger, chilies, lime zest, lime juice, 1 tablespoon of peanut oil, the fish sauce, cilantro, and basil in a food processor. Blend to a form a smooth paste, which should be of a spoonable consistency. If the sauce looks thick, add a little water. Remove and set aside.

2 Heat the wok, add the remaining 1 tablespoon of oil and, when hot, add the chicken. Stir-fry for 2–3 minutes until the chicken starts to color, then add the green beans and stir-fry for an additional 1 minute. Remove the chicken and beans from the wok and set aside. Wipe the wok clean with absorbent paper towels.

3 Spoon the reserved green paste into the wok and heat for 1 minute. Add the coconut milk and beat to blend. Return the chicken and beans to the wok

and bring to a boil. Simmer for 5–7 minutes or until the chicken is cooked. Sprinkle with basil leaves and serve immediately with freshly cooked rice.

TASTY TIP

Use Thai holy basil in this recipe if possible. The leaves are flatter and coarser than Italian basil with a stronger, more pronounced aniseed flavor. Thai basil is available from Asian grocery stores and some supermarkets.

CHICKEN CHOW MEIN

INGREDIENTS   Serves 4

3¼ cups egg noodles
5 tsp. sesame oil
4 tsp. light soy sauce
2 tbsp. Chinese rice wine or
   dry sherry
salt and freshly ground black
   pepper
½ lb. (225 g) skinless chicken
   breast fillets, cut into strips
3 tbsp. peanut oil
2 garlic cloves, peeled and
   finely chopped

½ cup snow peas, finely sliced
½ cup cooked ham, cut into
   fine strips
2 tsp. dark soy sauce
pinch of sugar

TO GARNISH:
shredded scallions
toasted sesame seeds

1 Bring a large saucepan of water to a boil and add the noodles. Cook for 3–5 minutes, drain and plunge into cold water. Drain again, add 1 tablespoon of the sesame oil and stir lightly.

2 Place 2 teaspoons of light soy sauce, 1 tablespoon of Chinese rice wine or sherry, and 1 teaspoon of the sesame oil, with seasoning to taste in a bowl. Add the chicken and stir well. Cover lightly and allow to marinate in the refrigerator for about 15 minutes.

3 Heat the wok over a high heat, add 1 tablespoon of the peanut oil and, when very hot, add the chicken and its marinade and stir-fry for 2 minutes. Remove the chicken and juices and set aside. Wipe the wok clean with absorbent paper towels.

4 Reheat the wok and add the oil. Add the garlic and toss in the oil for 20 seconds. Add the snow peas and the ham and stir-fry for 1 minute. Add the noodles, remaining light soy sauce, Chinese rice wine or sherry, the dark soy sauce, and sugar. Season to taste with salt and pepper and stir-fry for 2 minutes.

5 Add the chicken and juices to the wok and stir-fry for 4 minutes or until the chicken is cooked. Drizzle over the remaining sesame oil. Garnish with scallions and sesame seeds and serve.

FOOD FACT

Sesame oil is a thick, rich, golden brown oil made from toasted sesame seeds. It is used in Chinese cooking mainly as a seasoning.

CHICKEN SATAY SALAD

INGREDIENTS   Serves 4

4 tbsp. crunchy peanut butter
1 tbsp. chili sauce
1 garlic clove, peeled and
   crushed
2 tbsp. vinegar
2 tbsp. light soy sauce
2 tbsp. dark soy sauce
2 tsp. brown sugar
pinch of salt
2 tsp. freshly ground Sichuan
   or black peppercorns

6⅔ cups dried egg noodles
2 tbsp. sesame oil
1 tbsp. peanut oil
1 lb. (450 g) skinless, boneless
   chicken breast fillets, cut
   into cubes
shredded celery leaves, to
   garnish
romaine lettuce, to serve

1 Place the peanut butter, chili sauce, garlic, vinegar, soy sauces, sugar, salt, and ground peppercorns in a food processor and blend to form a smooth paste. Scrape into a bowl, cover with plastic wrap and chill in the refrigerator until required.

2 Bring a large saucepan of lightly salted water to a boil. Add the noodles and cook for 3–5 minutes. Drain and plunge into cold water. Drain again and toss in the sesame oil. Let cool.

3 Heat the wok until very hot, add the oil and, when hot, add the chicken cubes. Stir-fry for 5–6 minutes until the chicken is golden brown and cooked through.

4 Remove the chicken from the wok using a slotted spoon and add to the noodles,

together with the peanut sauce. Mix lightly together, then sprinkle with the shredded celery leaves and either serve immediately or leave until cold, then serve with romaine lettuce.

FOOD FACT

Sichuan peppercorns are the dried berries of a shrub, which is a member of the citrus family. The smell is reminiscent of lavender and they have a sharp, mildly spicy flavor. They are often toasted in a dry skillet before grinding, to bring out their distinctive flavor.

DUCK IN CRISPY WON TON SHELLS

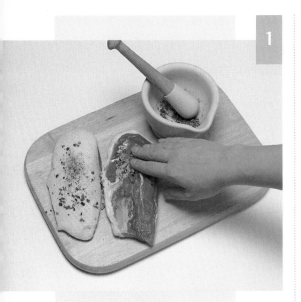

INGREDIENTS   Serves 4

2 duck breasts	1 tbsp. cornstarch
2 tbsp. Chinese five spice powder	3 cups vegetable oil for deep-frying
2 tbsp. Sichuan peppercorns	16 won ton wrappers
1 tsp. whole black peppercorns	2 in. (5 cm) piece cucumber, cut into fine strips
3 tbsp. cumin seeds	½ cup hoisin or plum sauce
5 tbsp. sea salt	
6 slices fresh ginger	
6 scallions, coarsely chopped	

1 Rinse the duck and dry thoroughly with absorbent paper towels. Place the Chinese five spice powder, peppercorns, cumin seeds, and salt in a mortar and pestle and crush. Rub the spice mix all over the duck. Wrap in plastic wrap and refrigerate for 24 hours.

2 Place a rack in the wok and pour in boiling water to a depth of 2 inches (5 cm). Place the duck breasts with the ginger slices and 3 chopped scallions in a heatproof dish on top of the rack. Cover and steam for 40–50 minutes or until the duck is cooked. Pour off any excess fat from time to time and add more water if necessary. Remove the duck and leave until cooled.

3 Dust the duck breasts with cornstarch, shaking off the excess. Heat the wok, add the oil and, when almost smoking, deep-fry the duck for 8 minutes. Drain, then shred the meat into bite-sized pieces. Shred the remaining scallions.

4 Reheat the oil until smoking. Working with one won ton at a time, insert 2 wooden skewers or toothpicks into each one, hold in a taco shape and lower into the oil. Hold in the oil until crisp and golden. Drain on paper towels. Repeat with the remaining won tons. Fill the won tons with the duck, topped with the scallions, cucumber, and hoisin sauce. Serve immediately.

FOOD FACT

Chinese five spice powder contains star anise, Sichuan pepper, fennel, cloves, and cinnamon.

CHICKEN & BABY VEGETABLE STIR FRY

INGREDIENTS

Serves 4

2 tbsp. peanut oil

1 small red chili, seeded and finely chopped

⅓ lb. (150 g) chicken breast or thigh meat, skinned and cut into cubes

2 baby leeks, trimmed and sliced

12 asparagus spears, halved

1 cup snow peas, trimmed

1 cup baby carrots, trimmed and halved lengthwise

¾ cup fine green beans, trimmed and diagonally sliced

1 cup baby corn, diagonally halved

¼ cup chicken stock

2 tsp. light soy sauce

1 tbsp. dry sherry

1 tsp. sesame oil

toasted sesame seeds, to garnish

1 Heat the wok until very hot and add the oil. Add the chopped chili and chicken and stir-fry for 4–5 minutes or until the chicken is cooked and golden.

2 Increase the heat, add the leeks to the chicken and stir-fry for 2 minutes. Add the asparagus spears, snow peas, baby carrots, green beans, and baby corn. Stir-fry for 3–4 minutes or until the vegetables soften slightly but still retain a slight crispness.

3 In a small bowl, mix together the chicken stock, soy sauce, dry sherry, and sesame oil. Pour into the wok, stir and cook until

heated through. Sprinkle with the toasted sesame seeds and serve immediately.

HELPFUL HINT

Look for packages of mixed baby vegetables in the super-market. They are often available ready trimmed and will save a lot of time.

SWEET-&-SOUR TURKEY

INGREDIENTS   Serves 4

2 tbsp. peanut oil
2 garlic cloves, peeled and
  chopped
1 tbsp. freshly grated ginger
4 scallions, trimmed and cut
  into 1½ in. (4 cm) lengths
1 lb. (450 g) turkey breast,
  skinned and cut into strips
1 red bell pepper, seeded
  and cut into 1 in. (2.5 cm)
  squares

8 oz. (225 g) can water
  chestnuts, drained
⅔ cup chicken stock
2 tbsp. Chinese rice wine
3 tbsp. light soy sauce
2 tsp. dark soy sauce
2 tbsp. tomato paste
2 tbsp. white wine vinegar
1 tbsp. sugar
1 tbsp. cornstarch
egg-fried rice, to serve

1 Heat the wok over a high heat, add the oil and, when hot, add the garlic, ginger, and scallions, stir-fry for about 20 seconds.

2 Add the turkey to the wok and stir-fry for 2 minutes or until beginning to color. Add the bell peppers and water chestnuts and stir-fry for an additional 2 minutes.

3 Mix the chicken stock, Chinese rice wine, light and dark soy sauce, tomato paste, white wine vinegar, and the sugar together in a small jug or bowl. Add the mixture to the wok, stir and bring the sauce to a boil.

4 Mix together the cornstarch with 2 tablespoons of water and add to the wok. Reduce the heat and simmer for 3 minutes or until the turkey is cooked

thoroughly and the sauce slightly thickened and glossy. Serve immediately with egg-fried rice.

TASTY TIP

To make egg-fried rice, heat 1 tablespoon vegetable oil in a clean wok. Add 5 cups cold cooked rice and stir-fry briefly before adding 1 cup thawed frozen peas. Stir-fry for an additional 5 minutes over a high heat. Add 2 medium beaten eggs and ¾ cup beansprouts and cook for an additional 2 minutes until the eggs have set. Turn the mixture onto a plate and garnish with 2 finely chopped scallions. Serve immediately.

THAI COCONUT CHICKEN

INGREDIENTS   Serves 4

1 tsp. cumin seeds
1 tsp. mustard seeds
1 tsp. coriander seeds
1 tsp. turmeric
1 bird's eye chili, seeded and
   finely chopped
1 tbsp. freshly grated ginger
2 garlic cloves, peeled and
   finely chopped
½ cup heavy cream
8 skinless chicken thighs
2 tbsp. peanut oil

1 onion, peeled and finely
   sliced
1 cup coconut milk
salt and freshly ground black
   pepper
4 tbsp. freshly chopped
   cilantro
2 scallions, shredded,
   to garnish
freshly cooked Thai fragrant
   rice, to serve

1 Heat the wok and add the cumin seeds, mustard seeds, and coriander seeds. Dry-fry over a low to medium heat for 2 minutes or until the fragrance becomes stronger and the seeds start to pop. Add the turmeric and let cool slightly. Grind the spices in a mortar and pestle or blend to a fine powder in a food processor.

2 Mix the chili, ginger, garlic, and the cream together in a small bowl, add the ground spices and mix. Place the chicken thighs in a shallow dish and spread the spice paste over the thighs.

3 Heat the wok over a high heat, add the oil and, when hot, add the onion and stir-fry until golden brown. Add the chicken and spice paste. Cook for 5–6 minutes, stirring occasionally until evenly colored. Add the

coconut milk and season to taste with salt and pepper. Simmer the chicken for 15–20 minutes or until the thighs are cooked through, taking care not to allow the mixture to boil. Stir in the chopped cilantro and serve immediately with the freshly cooked rice sprinkled with shredded scallions.

TASTY TIP

Dry-frying the spices before grinding them helps to release their essential oils. This, in turn, brings out the flavor of the spices, making them much more aromatic.

DEEP-FRIED CHICKEN WINGS

INGREDIENTS   Serves 4

2 tsp. turmeric
1 tsp. hot chili powder
1 tsp. ground coriander
1 tsp. ground cumin
3 garlic cloves, peeled and
  crushed
8 chicken wings
2 tbsp. orange marmalade
2 tbsp. ginger jelly or
  marmalade
1 tsp. salt

3 tbsp. rice wine vinegar
2 tbsp. tomato ketchup
3 cups vegetable oil for
  deep-frying
lime wedges, to garnish

1 Blend the turmeric, chili powder, ground coriander, ground cumin, and garlic together in a small bowl. Dry the chicken wings thoroughly, using absorbent paper towels, then rub the spice mixture onto the skin of each chicken wing. Cover and chill in the refrigerator for at least 2 hours.

2 Meanwhile make the dipping sauce, by mixing together the marmalade, ginger jelly, salt, rice wine vinegar, and tomato ketchup in a small saucepan. Heat until blended, let cool, then serve. If using straightaway, spoon into a small dipping bowl but if using later pour into a container with a close-fitting lid and store in the refrigerator.

3 Pour the oil into the wok and heat to 375° F (190° C) or until a small cube of bread dropped in the oil turns golden brown in 30

seconds. Cook 2–3 chicken wings at a time, lowering them into the hot oil, and deep-frying for 3–4 minutes. Remove the wings, using a slotted spoon, and drain on absorbent paper towels. You may need to reheat the oil before cooking each batch.

4 When all the chicken wings are cooked, arrange on a warmed serving dish, garnish with the lime wedges and serve.

HELPFUL HINT

It is important to test the oil to make sure it is at the right temperature. If the oil is not hot enough, the chicken will be greasy but if it is too hot, the food may burn on the outside without being properly cooked through.

STIR-FRIED CHICKEN WITH BASIL

INGREDIENTS   Serves 4

3 tbsp. corn oil
3 tbsp. green curry paste
1 lb. (450 g) skinless, boneless
   chicken breast fillets,
   trimmed and cut into cubes
8 cherry tomatoes
½ cup coconut cream
2 tbsp. brown sugar
2 tbsp. Thai fish sauce
1 red chili, seeded and
   thinly sliced

1 green chlli, seeded and
   thinly sliced
6 tbsp. fresh torn basil leaves
sprigs of fresh cilantro, to
   garnish
freshly steamed white rice,
   to serve

1 Heat the wok, then add the oil and heat for 1 minute. Add the green curry paste and cook, stirring for 1 minute to release the flavor and cook the paste. Add the chicken and stir-fry over a high heat for 2 minutes, making sure the chicken is coated thoroughly with the green curry paste.

2 Reduce the heat under the wok, then add the cherry tomatoes and cook, stirring gently for 2–3 minutes or until the tomatoes burst and begin to disintegrate into the green curry paste.

3 Add half the coconut cream and add to the wok with the brown sugar, Thai fish sauce, and the red and green chilies. Stir-fry gently for 5 minutes or until the sauce is amalgamated and the chicken is cooked thoroughly.

4 Just before serving, sprinkle the chicken with the torn basil leaves and add the remaining coconut cream, then serve immediately with freshly steamed white rice garnished with fresh cilantro sprigs.

FOOD FACT

Creamed coconut is a waxy block of hardened coconut cream. It is very high in fat but adds a rich creaminess to the dish. It can be chopped or shredded and melts easily on contact with the hot sauce.

NOODLES WITH TURKEY & MUSHROOMS

INGREDIENTS   Serves 4

3¼ cups dried egg noodles
1 tbsp. peanut oil
1 red onion, peeled and sliced
2 tbsp. freshly grated ginger
3 garlic cloves, peeled and
  finely chopped
¾ lb. (350 g) turkey
  breast, skinned and
  cut into strips

1¼ cups chestnut mushrooms
1 cup baby button mushrooms
2 tbsp. dark soy sauce
2 tbsp. hoisin or plum sauce
2 tbsp. dry sherry
4 tbsp. vegetable stock
2 tsp. cornstarch

1 Bring a large saucepan of lightly salted water to a boil and add the noodles. Cook for 3–5 minutes, then drain and plunge immediately into cold water. When cool, drain again and set aside.

2 Heat the wok, add the oil and, when hot, add the onion and stir-fry for 3 minutes until it starts to soften. Add the ginger and garlic and stir-fry for an additional 3 minutes, then add the turkey strips and stir-fry for 4–5 minutes until sealed and golden brown.

3 Wipe and slice the chestnut mushrooms into similar-sized pieces and add to the wok with the button mushrooms. Stir-fry for 3–4 minutes or until tender. When all the vegetables are tender and the turkey is cooked, add the soy sauce, hoisin sauce, sherry, and vegetable stock.

4 Mix the cornstarch with 2 tablespoons of water and add to the wok, then cook, stirring until the sauce thickens. Add the drained noodles to the wok, then toss the mixture together and serve immediately.

HELPFUL HINT

When buying wild mushrooms, choose dry looking specimens without any soft spots. To prepare them, do not wash but brush away any dirt and wipe over gently with a damp cloth.

CHICKEN & CASHEWS

INGREDIENTS

Serves 4

1 lb. (450 g) skinless chicken, boneless breast fillets, cut into ½ in. (1 cm) cubes
1 medium egg white, beaten
1 tsp. salt
1 tsp. sesame oil
2 tsp. cornstarch
1 cup peanut oil for deep frying
2 tsp. corn oil
½ cup unsalted cashews

4 scallions, shredded
½ cup snow peas, diagonally sliced
1 tbsp. Chinese rice wine
1 tbsp. light soy sauce
shredded scallions, to garnish
freshly steamed white rice with fresh cilantro leaves, to serve

1 Place the cubes of chicken in a large bowl. Add the egg white, salt, sesame oil, and cornstarch. Mix well to ensure the chicken is coated thoroughly. Chill in the refrigerator for 20 minutes.

2 Heat the wok until very hot, add the peanut oil and, when hot, remove the wok from the heat and add the chicken. Stir continuously to prevent the chicken from sticking to the wok. When the chicken turns white, after about 2 minutes, remove it using a slotted spoon and set aside. Discard the oil.

3 Wipe the wok clean with absorbent paper towels and heat it again until very hot. Add the corn oil and heat. When the oil is hot, add the cashews, scallions, and snow peas and stir-fry for 1 minute.

4 Add the rice wine and soy sauce. Return the chicken to the wok and stir-fry for 2 minutes. Garnish with shredded scallions and serve immediately with freshly steamed rice sprinkled with fresh cilantro.

FOOD FACT

Adding egg white mixed with cornstarch to raw chicken is a classic Chinese technique called "velveting." It makes the chicken particularly tender. However, the egg white tends to stick to the wok, so the wok usually needs to be wiped clean between the different stages of cooking.

SICHUAN TURKEY NOODLES

INGREDIENTS · Serves 4

1 tbsp. tomato paste
2 tsp. black bean sauce
2 tsp. vinegar
salt and freshly ground black pepper
½ tsp. Sichuan pepper
2 tsp. sugar
4 tsp. sesame oil
3¼ cups dried egg noodles
2 tbsp. peanut oil
2 tsp. freshly grated ginger

3 garlic cloves, peeled and coarsely chopped
2 shallots, peeled and finely chopped
2 zucchini, trimmed and cut into fine matchsticks
1 lb. (450 g) turkey breast, skinned and cut into strips
deep-fried onion rings, to garnish

1 Mix together the tomato paste, black bean sauce, vinegar, a pinch of salt and pepper, the sugar, and half the sesame oil. Chill in the refrigerator for 30 minutes.

2 Bring a large saucepan of lightly salted water to a boil and add the noodles. Cook for 3–5 minutes, drain and plunge immediately into cold water. Toss with the remaining sesame oil and set aside.

3 Heat the wok until very hot, then add the oil and, when hot, add the ginger, garlic, and shallots. Stir-fry for 20 seconds, then add the zucchini and turkey strips. Stir-fry for 3–4 minutes or until the turkey strips are sealed.

4 Add the prepared chilled black bean sauce and continue to stir-fry for another 4 minutes over a high heat. Add the drained noodles to the wok and stir until the noodles, turkey, vegetables, and the sauce are well mixed together. Garnish with the deep-fried onion rings and serve immediately.

FOOD FACT

Fresh ginger is indispensable as a flavoring in Chinese cookery. Its pungent, spicy, fresh taste adds a subtle but very distinctive flavor to all types of dishes. Ginger looks rather like a gnarled Jerusalem artichoke and can vary in size. It has a pale brown, papery skin that is usually removed before use. Look for firm pieces with no signs of shriveling. Keep ginger wrapped in plastic wrap in the refrigerator.

STIR-FRIED CHICKEN WITH SPINACH, TOMATOES, & PINE NUTS

INGREDIENTS
Serves 4

½ cup pine nuts
2 tbsp. corn oil
1 red onion, peeled and finely chopped
1 lb. (450 g) skinless, boneless chicken breast fillets, cut into strips
4 cups cherry tomatoes, halved
5 cups baby spinach, washed

salt and freshly ground black pepper
¼ tsp. freshly grated nutmeg
2 tbsp. balsamic vinegar
⅓ cup cup raisins
freshly cooked ribbon noodles tossed in butter, to serve

1 Heat the wok and add the pine nuts. Dry-fry for about 2 minutes, shaking often to ensure that they toast but do not burn. Remove and set aside. Wipe any dust from the wok.

2 Heat the wok again, add the oil and, when hot, add the red onion and stir-fry for 2 minutes. Add the chicken and stir-fry for 2–3 minutes or until golden brown. Reduce the heat, toss in the cherry tomatoes and stir-fry gently until the tomatoes start to disintegrate.

3 Add the baby spinach and stir-fry for 2–3 minutes or until they start to wilt. Season to taste with salt and pepper, then sprinkle in the grated nutmeg and drizzle with the balsamic vinegar. Finally, stir in the raisins

and reserved toasted pine nuts. Serve immediately on a bed of buttered ribbon noodles.

HELPFUL HINT

Baby spinach is available ready to use in bags, sold in most supermarkets. It has a more subtle, creamier flavor than larger-leaved spinach and cooks very quickly.

LIME & SESAME TURKEY

INGREDIENTS
Serves 4

1 lb. (450 g) turkey breast, skinned and cut into strips

2 lemon grass stalks, outer leaves discarded and finely sliced

2 tsp. grated lime zest

4 garlic cloves, peeled and crushed

6 shallots, peeled and finely sliced

2 tbsp. Thai fish sauce

2 tsp. brown sugar

1 small red chlli, seeded and finely sliced

3 tbsp. corn oil

1 tbsp. sesame oil

3¼ cups stir-fry rice noodles

1 tbsp. sesame seeds

shredded scallions, to garnish

freshly stir-fried vegetables, to serve

1 Place the turkey strips in a shallow dish. Mix together the lemon grass stalks, lime zest, garlic, shallots, Thai fish sauce, sugar, and chili with 2 tablespoons of the corn oil and the sesame oil. Pour over the turkey. Cover and allow to marinate in the refrigerator for 2–3 hours, spooning the marinade over the turkey occasionally.

2 Soak the noodles in warm water for 5 minutes. Drain through a strainer, then plunge immediately into cold water. Drain again and set aside until ready to use.

3 Heat the wok until very hot and add the sesame seeds. Dry-fry for 1–2 minutes or until toasted in color. Remove from the wok and set aside. Wipe the wok to remove any dust left from the seeds.

4 Heat the wok again and add the remaining corn oil. When hot, drain the turkey from the marinade and stir-fry for 3–4 minutes or until golden brown and cooked through (you may need to do this in 2 batches). When all the turkey has been cooked, add the noodles to the wok and cook, stirring, for 1–2 minutes or until heated through thoroughly. Garnish with the shredded scallions, toasted sesame seeds, and serve immediately with freshly stir-fried vegetables of your choice.

FOOD FACT

Lemon grass is a common ingredient in Thai cooking. It looks a little like a scallion but has a distinctive lemony flavor. It keeps well for two to three weeks in the refrigerator.

HOISIN DUCK & GREENS STIR FRY

INGREDIENTS
Serves 4

¾ lb. (350 g) duck breasts, skinned and cut into strips
1 medium egg white, beaten
½ tsp. salt
1 tsp. sesame oil
2 tsp. cornstarch
2 tbsp. peanut oil
2 tbsp. freshly grated ginger
⅓ cup bamboo shoots
½ cup fine green beans, trimmed

1¼ cups bok choy, trimmed
2 tbsp. hoisin or plum sauce
1 tsp. Chinese rice wine or dry sherry
3 tsp. grated orange zest
1 tbsp. orange juice
strips of orange zest, to garnish
freshly steamed egg noodles, to serve

1 Place the duck strips in a shallow dish, then add the egg white, salt, sesame oil, and cornstarch. Stir lightly until the duck is coated in the mixture. Cover and chill in the refrigerator for 20 minutes.

2 Heat the wok until very hot and add the oil. Remove the wok from the heat and add the duck, stirring continuously to prevent the duck from sticking to the wok. Add the ginger and stir-fry for 2 minutes. Add the bamboo shoots, the green beans, and the bok choy and stir-fry for 1–2 minutes until wilted.

3 Mix together the hoisin sauce, the Chinese rice wine or sherry, the orange zest, and orange juice. Pour into the wok and stir to coat the duck and vegetables. Stir-fry for 1–2 minutes or until the duck and vegetables are tender. Garnish with the strips of orange zest and serve immediately with freshly steamed egg noodles.

HELPFUL HINT

Duck breasts are usually sold with the skin on but it is very easy to remove and all the fat usually comes away readily with the skin. If any remains, simply remove with a sharp knife.

DUCK & EXOTIC FRUIT STIR FRY

INGREDIENTS   Serves 4

4 duck breast fillets, skinned
  removed and cut into strips
½ tsp. Chinese five spice
  powder
2 tbsp. soy sauce
1 tbsp. sesame oil
1 tbsp. peanut oil
2 celery stalks, trimmed and
  diced
8 oz. (225 g) can pineapples
  chunks, drained

1 mango, peeled, pitted, and
  cut into chunks
¾ cup litchis, peeled if fresh,
  pitted, and halved
½ cup chicken stock
2 tbsp. tomato paste
2 tbsp. plum sauce
2 tsp. wine vinegar
pinch of brown sugar
toasted nuts, to garnish
steamed rice, to serve

1 Place the duck strips in a shallow bowl. Mix together the Chinese five spice powder, soy sauce, and sesame oil. Pour over the duck and marinate for 2 hours in the refrigerator. Stir occasionally during marinating. Remove the duck from the marinade and set aside.

2 Heat the wok, add the oil and, when hot, stir-fry the marinated duck strips for 4 minutes. Remove from the wok and set aside.

3 Add the celery to the wok and stir-fry for 2 minutes, then add the pineapple, mango, and litchis and stir-fry for an additional 3 minutes. Return the duck to the wok.

4 Mix together the chicken stock, tomato paste, plum sauce, wine vinegar, and a pinch of brown sugar. Add to the wok,

bring to a boil and simmer, stirring for 2 minutes. Sprinkle with the nuts and serve immediately with the freshly steamed rice.

TASTY TIP

The exotic fruit in this recipe not only looks beautiful but helps to cut through the richness of the duck meat. Do not overcook the duck or it will become dry.

Teriyaki Duck with Plum Chutney

INGREDIENTS
Serves 4

4 tbsp. Japanese soy sauce

4 tbsp. dry sherry

2 garlic cloves, peeled and finely chopped

1 in. (2.5 cm) piece fresh ginger, peeled and finely chopped

¾ lb. (350 g) skinless duck breast fillets, cut in chunks

2 tbsp. peanut oil

1½ cups carrots, peeled and cut into fine strips

½ cucumber, cut into strips

5 scallions, trimmed and shredded

toasted almonds, to garnish

freshly cooked egg noodles, to serve

FOR THE PLUM CHUTNEY:

¼ stick butter

1 red onion, peeled and finely chopped

2 tsp. brown sugar

4 plums, pitted and halved

3 tsp. grated orange zest

1 tbsp. orange juice

⅓ cup raisins

1 Mix together the soy sauce, sherry, garlic, and ginger and pour into a shallow dish. Add the duck strips and stir until coated in the marinade. Cover and leave in the refrigerator for 30 minutes.

2 Meanwhile make the plum chutney. Melt the butter in a wok, add the onion and sugar and cook gently over a low heat for 20 minutes. Add the plums, orange zest, and juice and simmer for 10 minutes, then stir in the raisins. Spoon into a bowl and wipe the wok clean. Drain the duck, setting aside the marinade.

3 Heat the wok, add the oil and, when hot, add the carrots, cucumber, and scallions. Stir-fry for 2 minutes or until tender. Remove and set aside.

4 Add the drained duck to the wok and stir-fry over a high heat for 2 minutes. Return the vegetables to the wok and add the reserved marinade. Stir-fry briefly until heated through.

5 Garnish the duck with the toasted almonds and serve immediately with freshly cooked noodles and the plum chutney.

HELPFUL HINT

If the plum chutney is a bit runny, bring to a boil and cook for 5 minutes to thicken.

STEAMED, CRISPY, CITRUS CHICKEN

INGREDIENTS
Serves 6

¾ cup light soy sauce
1 tbsp. brown sugar
4 star anise
2 slices fresh ginger, peeled
5 scallions, trimmed and
  sliced
1 small orange, cut into
  wedges
1 lime, cut into wedges
2½ lb. (1.1 kg) chicken

2 garlic cloves, peeled and
  finely chopped
2 tbsp. Chinese rice wine
2 tbsp. dark soy sauce
1 cup peanut oil
orange slices, to garnish
freshly cooked steamed rice,
  to serve

1 Pour the light soy sauce and ¾ cup of water into the wok and add the sugar, and star anise. Bring to a boil over a gentle heat. Pour into a small bowl and let cool slightly. Wipe the wok clean with absorbent paper towels.

2 Put the ginger, 2 scallions, orange, and lime inside the cavity of the chicken. Place a rack in the wok and pour in boiling water to a depth of 2 inches (5 cm). Put a piece of foil onto the rack and place the chicken in the center, then pour over the soy sauce mixture.

3 Cover the wok and steam gently for 1–1 hour 10 minutes or until the chicken is cooked through, pouring off excess fat from time to time. Add more water if necessary. Let the chicken cool and dry for up to 3 hours, then cut the chicken into quarters.

4 Mix together the garlic, Chinese rice wine, dark soy sauce, and remaining scallions, then set aside. Dry the wok and heat again, then add the oil. When hot, pan-fry the chicken quarters for 4 minutes or until golden and crisp. Do this one portion at a time, remove and drain on paper towels.

5 When cool enough to handle shred into bite-sized pieces and drizzle over the sauce. Garnish with slices of orange and serve with freshly steamed rice.

TASTY TIP

If you prefer, serve the shredded chicken with ready-made Chinese pancakes, which have been spread with a little hoisin sauce. Top with shredded scallions and cucumber and roll up.

THAI SPRING ROLLS WITH NOODLES & DIPPING SAUCE

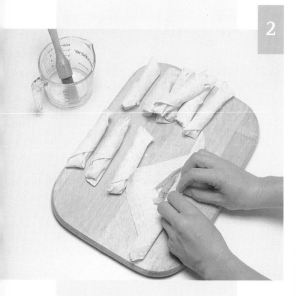

INGREDIENTS   Makes about 30

1 cup dried rice vermicelli

1 carrot, peeled and cut into matchsticks

½ cup snow peas, thinly shredded lengthwise

3 scallions, trimmed and finely chopped

1 cup shelled shrimp, thawed if frozen

2 garlic cloves, peeled and crushed

1 tsp. sesame oil

2 tbsp. light soy sauce

1 tsp. chili sauce

½ lb. (225 g) phyllo pastry, cut into 6 in. (15 cm) squares

1 medium egg white, lightly beaten

vegetable oil for deep-frying

sprigs of fresh cilantro, to garnish

sweet chili sauce for dipping

1 Cook the rice vermicelli according to the package directions, then drain thoroughly. Coarsely chop and set aside. Bring a saucepan of lightly salted water to a boil and blanch the carrot and snow peas for 1 minute. Drain and refresh under cold water, then drain again and pat dry on absorbent paper towels. Mix together with the noodles. Add the scallions, shrimp, garlic, sesame oil, soy and chili sauces, and set aside.

2 Fold the phyllo pastry squares in half diagonally to form triangles. Lay a triangle with the fold facing you and place a spoonful of the mixture in the center. Roll over the long end of the wrapper to enclose the filling, then bring over the corners to enclose the ends of the roll. Brush the point of the spring roll furthest from you with a little beaten egg white and continue rolling to seal.

3 Fill a wok about one third full with vegetable oil and heat to 375° F (190° C) or until a cube of bread browns in 30 seconds. Deep-fry the spring rolls, 4 or 5 at a time for 1–2 minutes or until golden and crisp. Drain on absorbent paper towels. Fry the remaining spring rolls in batches. Garnish with sprigs of cilantro and serve hot with the dark soy sauce and sweet chili sauce.

HELPFUL HINT

If available, use spring roll wrappers instead of phyllo pastry. Buy the larger sized ones and follow the recipe from step 2.

SINGAPORE NOODLES

INGREDIENTS   Serves 4

2⅔ cups flat rice noodles
3 tbsp. corn oil
2 shallots, peeled and sliced
2 garlic cloves, peeled and crushed
2 tbsp. freshly shredded ginger
1 red bell pepper, seeded and finely sliced
1 hot red chili, seeded and finely chopped

1½ cups shelled raw shrimp
1¼ cups boneless pork, diced
2 cups boneless chicken, diced
1 tbsp. curry powder
1 tsp. each crushed fennel seeds and ground cinnamon
½ cup frozen peas, thawed
3 tbsp. lemon juice
3 tbsp. fresh cilantro leaves

1 Put the noodles into a large bowl and pour over boiling water to cover. Allow to stand for 3 minutes or until slightly underdone according to the package directions. Drain well and set aside.

2 Heat a wok until almost smoking. Add the oil and carefully swirl to coat the sides of the wok. Add the shallots, garlic, and ginger and cook for a few seconds. Add the bell pepper and chili and stir-fry for 3–4 minutes or until the pepper has softened.

3 Add the shrimp, pork, chicken, and curry powder to the wok. Stir-fry for an additional 4–5 minutes until the meat and shrimp are colored on all sides. Then add the fennel seeds and the cinnamon and stir to mix.

4 Add the drained noodles to the wok along with the peas and cook for an additional 1–2 minutes until heated through. Add the lemon juice to taste. Sprinkle with the fresh cilantro leaves and serve immediately.

HELPFUL HINT

Use whatever meat or fish you prefer according to taste. This is also a great dish for using up leftover meat, perhaps from the Sunday dinner. If using cooked meat, reduce the cooking time accordingly but ensure that it is piping hot.

EASTERN NOODLE & PEANUT SALAD WITH CILANTRO

INGREDIENTS   Serves 4

4¼ cups rice vermicelli
4 cups light chicken stock
2 tsp. sesame oil
2 tbsp. light soy sauce
8 scallions
3 tbsp. peanut oil
2 hot green chilies, seeded
  and thinly sliced
1 tbsp. coarsely chopped
  cilantro
2 tbsp. freshly chopped mint

¼ cucumber, finely chopped
⅓ cup beansprouts
⅓ cup roasted peanuts,
  coarsely chopped

1 Put the noodles into a large bowl. Bring the stock to a boil and immediately pour over the noodles. Let soak for 4 minutes or according to the package directions. Drain well, discarding the stock or saving it for another use. Mix together the sesame oil and soy sauce and pour over the hot noodles. Toss well to coat and leave until cold.

2 Trim and thinly slice 4 of the scallions. Heat the oil in a wok over a low heat. Add the scallions and, as soon as they sizzle, remove from the heat and let cool. When cold, toss with the noodles.

3 On a chopping board, cut the remaining scallions lengthwise 4–6 times, leave in a bowl of cold water until tassels form. Serve the noodles in individual bowls, each dressed with a little chili, cilantro, mint, cucumber, beansprouts, and peanuts. Garnish with the scallion tassels and serve.

HELPFUL HINT

To make this dish entirely vegetarian, cook the noodles in vegetable stock or water. If using water, be sure to add salt.

JAMBALAYAN-STYLE FRIED RICE

INGREDIENTS   Serves 6

2 cups long-grain rice
3 cups hot chicken or fish
  stock
2 fresh bay leaves
2 tbsp. vegetable oil
2 medium onions, peeled and
  coarsely chopped
1 green bell pepper, seeded
  and coarsely chopped
2 celery stalks, trimmed and
  coarsely chopped
3 garlic cloves, peeled and
  finely chopped
1 tsp. dried oregano

¾ lb. (350 g) skinless chicken
  breast fillets, chopped
1 cup chorizo or similar spicy
  sausage, chopped
3 tomatoes, peeled and
  chopped
12 large raw shrimp, shelled
  if preferred
4 scallions, trimmed and finely
  chopped
2 tbsp. freshly chopped
  parsley
salt and freshly ground black
  pepper

1 Put the rice, stock, and bay leaves into a large saucepan and bring to a boil. Cover with a tight-fitting lid and simmer for 10 minutes over a very low heat. Remove from the heat and leave for an additional 10 minutes.

2 Meanwhile heat a large wok, then add the oil and heat. When hot, add the onions, green bell pepper, celery, garlic, and oregano. Stir-fry for 6 minutes or until all the vegetables have softened. Add the chicken and chorizo and stir-fry for an additional 6 minutes or until lightly browned.

3 Add the tomatoes and cook over a medium heat for 2–3 minutes until collapsed. Then stir in the shrimp and cook for an additional 4 minutes or until they are cooked through. Stir in the cooked rice, scallions and chopped parsley, and season to taste with salt and pepper. Serve immediately.

TASTY TIP

Look for large, fat chorizo for this dish. The small, thin sausages are not authentic and have less flavor.

Chicken & Red Bell Pepper Curried Rice

INGREDIENTS   Serves 4

1½ cups long-grain rice
salt
1 large egg white
1 tbsp. cornstarch
¾ lb. (350 g) skinless chicken
 breast fillets, cut into chunks
3 tbsp. peanut oil
1 red bell pepper, seeded and
 coarsely chopped
1 tbsp. curry powder or paste
½ cup chicken stock

1 tsp. sugar
1 tbsp. Chinese rice wine or
 dry sherry
1 tbsp. light soy sauce
sprigs of fresh cilantro, to
 garnish

1 Wash the rice in several changes of water until the water remains relatively clear. Drain well. Put into a saucepan and cover with fresh water. Add a little salt and bring to a boil. Cook for 7–8 minutes until tender. Drain and refresh under cold running water, then drain again and set aside.

2 Lightly beat the egg white with 1 teaspoon of salt and 2 teaspoons of cornstarch until smooth. Add the chicken and mix together well. Cover and chill in the refrigerator for 20 minutes.

3 Heat the oil in a wok until moderately hot. Add the chicken mixture to the wok and stir-fry for 2–3 minutes until all the chicken has turned white. Using a slotted spoon, lift the

cubes of chicken from the wok, then drain on absorbent paper towels.

4 Add the red bell pepper to the wok and stir-fry for 1 minute over a high heat. Add the curry powder and cook for 30 seconds, then add the chicken stock, sugar, Chinese rice wine, and soy sauce.

5 Mix the remaining cornstarch with 1 teaspoon of cold water and add to the wok, stirring. Bring to a boil and simmer gently for 1 minute.

6 Return the chicken to the wok, then simmer for an additional 1 minute before adding the rice. Stir over a medium heat for another 2 minutes until heated through. Garnish with the sprigs of cilantro and serve.

CHAR SUI PORK & NOODLE SALAD

INGREDIENTS
Serves 4

1¾ cups flat rice noodles
4 tbsp. molasses
2 tbsp. dark soy sauce
3 tbsp. Chinese rice wine or
  dry sherry
3 star anise, coarsely crushed
1 cinnamon stick
¾ lb. (350 g) pork tenderloin, in
  1 piece
1 tbsp. peanut oil
2 garlic cloves, peeled and
  finely chopped

1 tsp. freshly grated ginger
3 scallions, trimmed
  and sliced
1½ cups bok choy, coarsely
  chopped
2 tbsp. light soy sauce
fresh cilantro leaves, to
  garnish
prepared or bought plum
  sauce (see page 172),
  to serve

1 Preheat the oven to 425° F (220° C), 15 minutes before cooking. Soak the noodles in boiling water according to the package directions. Drain and set aside. Place the molasses, soy sauce, Chinese rice wine or sherry, star anise, and cinnamon into a small saucepan and stir over a gentle heat until mixed thoroughly, then set aside.

2 Trim the pork tenderloin of any excess fat and put into a shallow dish. Pour the cooled sauce over the tenderloin. Turn the pork, making sure it is completely coated in the sauce. Place in the refrigerator and allow to marinate for 4 hours, turning occasionally.

3 Remove the pork from its marinade and transfer to a roasting pan. Roast in the preheated oven for 12–14 minutes, basting once until cooked through. Remove from the oven and leave until warm.

4 Heat the wok, add the oil and, when hot, add the garlic, ginger, and scallions. Stir-fry for 30 seconds before adding the bok choy. Stir-fry for an additional 1 minute until the bok choy has wilted, then add the noodles and soy sauce. Toss until mixed, then transfer to a large serving dish. Let cool.

5 Thickly slice the pork fillet and add to the cooled noodles. Garnish with cilantro leaves and serve with plum sauce.

TASTY TIP

In fine weather, the pork can be cooked on the barbecue for a pleasant smoky flavor.

THAI RICE CAKES WITH MANGO SALSA

INGREDIENTS   Serves 4

⅔ cup Thai fragrant rice

14 oz. (400 g) can coconut
  milk

1 lemon grass stalk, bruised

2 kaffir lime leaves, shredded

1 tbsp. vegetable oil, plus
  extra for deep-frying

1 garlic clove, peeled and
  finely chopped

1 tsp. freshly grated ginger

1 red bell pepper, seeded and
  finely chopped

2 red chilies, seeded and finely
  chopped

1 medium egg, beaten

¼ cup dried bread crumbs

FOR THE MANGO SALSA:

1 large mango, peeled, pitted,
  and finely chopped

1 small red onion, peeled and
  finely chopped

2 tbsp. freshly chopped
  cilantro

2 tbsp. freshly chopped basil

1 tbsp. lime juice

1 Wash the rice in several changes of water until the water stays relatively clear. Drain, place in a saucepan with a tight-fitting lid and add the coconut milk, lemon grass, and lime leaves. Bring to a boil, cover and cook over the lowest possible heat for 10 minutes. Turn off the heat and let stand for 10 minutes, without lifting the lid.

2 Heat the wok, then add 1 tablespoon of oil and, when hot, add the garlic, ginger, red bell pepper and half the chili. Stir-fry for 1–2 minutes until just softened, then place in a large bowl.

3 When the rice is cooked, turn into the bowl and add the egg. Season to taste with salt and pepper and mix together well. Put the bread crumbs into a shallow dish. Form the rice mixture into 8 cakes and coat them in the bread crumbs. Chill in the refrigerator for 30 minutes.

4 Meanwhile make the mango salsa. In a bowl, mix together the mango, red onion, cilantro, basil, lime juice, and remaining red chili and set aside

5 Fill a clean wok about one third full of vegetable oil. Heat to 375° F (190° C) or until a cube of bread browns in 30 seconds. Cook the rice cakes, 1 or 2 at a time for 2–3 minutes until golden and crisp. Drain on paper towels. Serve with the mango salsa.

FRAGRANT FRUIT PILAF

INGREDIENTS Serves 4–6

½ stick butter
6 green cardamom pods
1 cinnamon stick
2 bay leaves
2 cups basmati rice
2½ cups chicken stock
1 onion, peeled and finely
  chopped
½ cup slivered almonds
½ cup shelled pistachios,
  coarsely chopped

¾ cup dried figs, coarsely
  chopped
⅓ cup dried apricots, coarsely
  chopped
⅔ lb. (300 g) skinless chicken
  breast fillets, cut into chunks
salt and freshly ground black
  pepper
fresh parsley or cilantro
  leaves, to garnish

1 Melt half the butter in a saucepan or casserole dish with a tight-fitting lid. Add the cardamom pods and cinnamon stick and cook for about 30 seconds before adding the bay leaves and rice. Stir well to coat the rice in the butter and add the stock. Bring to a boil, cover tightly and cook very gently for 15 minutes. Remove from the heat and let stand for an additional 5 minutes.

2 Melt the remaining butter in a wok and when foaming, add the onion, almonds and pistachios. Stir-fry for 3–4 minutes until the nuts are beginning to brown. Remove and set aside.

3 Reduce the heat slightly and add the dried figs, apricots, and chicken and stir-fry for an additional 7–8 minutes until the chicken is cooked through. Return the nut mixture and toss to mix.

4 Remove from the heat, then remove the cinnamon stick and bay leaves. Add the cooked rice and stir together well to mix. Season to taste with salt and pepper. Garnish with parsley or cilantro leaves and serve immediately.

TASTY TIP

Leave the chicken out of this recipe, reducing the cooking time accordingly, to make a tasty side dish or vegetarian option.

RICE WITH SQUASH & SAGE

INGREDIENTS

Serves 4–6

1 lb. (450 g) butternut squash
¾ stick unsalted butter
1 small onion, peeled and finely chopped
3 garlic cloves, peeled and crushed
2 tbsp. freshly chopped sage
4 cups vegetable or chicken stock
2 cups risotto rice

½ cup pine nuts, toasted
¼ cup freshly shredded Parmesan cheese
freshly snipped chives, to garnish
salt and freshly ground black pepper

1 Peel the squash, cut in half lengthwise and remove seeds and stringy flesh. Cut remaining flesh into cubes and set aside.

2 Heat the wok, add the butter and heat until foaming, then add the onion, garlic, and sage and stir-fry for 1 minute.

3 Add the squash to the wok and stir-fry for an additional 10–12 minutes or until the squash is tender. Remove from the heat.

4 Meanwhile bring the vegetable or chicken stock to a boil and add the rice. Cook for 8–10 minutes or until the rice is just tender but still quite wet.

5 Add the cooked rice to the squash mixture. Stir in the pine nuts and Parmesan, season to taste with salt and pepper. Garnish with snipped chives and serve immediately.

FOOD FACT

Butternut squash are available most of the year and have a golden skin and a vibrant orange, well-flavored flesh, which is drier than pumpkin. Use the flesh as directed in the recipe.

BASMATI RICE WITH SAFFRON & FAVA BEANS

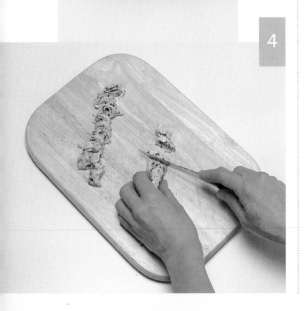

INGREDIENTS   Serves 4

1 medium egg
2 tbsp. olive oil
1 tbsp. freshly chopped mixed
  herbs
salt and freshly ground black
  pepper
1 cup basmati rice
½ stick butter
1 small onion, peeled and
  finely chopped

1 garlic clove, peeled and
  finely chopped
large pinch saffron strands
2⅔ cups shelled fava beans,
  blanched

1 Beat the egg with 1 teaspoon of olive oil and the herbs. Season lightly with salt and pepper. Heat the remaining teaspoon of olive oil in a wok or small skillet. Pour half the egg mixture into the wok, tilting it to coat the bottom. Cook gently until set on top. Flip over and cook for an additional 30 seconds. Transfer to a plate and repeat, using the remaining mixture, then set aside.

2 Wash the rice in several changes of water until the water remains relatively clear. Add the drained rice to a large saucepan of boiling salted water and cook for 12–15 minutes until tender. Drain well and set aside.

3 Heat the butter with the remaining oil in a wok and add the onion and garlic. Cook gently for 3–4 minutes until the onion is softened. Add the saffron and stir well. Add the drained rice and stir before adding the fava beans. Cook for an additional 2–3 minutes or until heated through.

4 Meanwhile roll the egg pancakes into cigar shapes then slice crosswise into strips. To serve, divide the rice among individual serving bowls and top with the egg strips.

FOOD FACT

Saffron is very expensive and is sold in tiny amounts. It adds a distinctive aroma, a buttery flavor and beautiful color to food it is cooked with. Before using, crush it lightly in a mortar and pestle.

THAI FRIED RICE WITH SHRIMP & CHILIES

INGREDIENTS

Serves 4

1 cup Thai fragrant rice

2 tbsp. peanut or vegetable oil

2 garlic cloves, peeled and finely chopped

2 red chilies, seeded and finely chopped

1 cup shelled raw shrimp

1 tbsp. Thai fish sauce

¼ tsp. sugar

1 tbsp. light soy sauce

½ small onion, peeled and finely sliced

½ red bell pepper, seeded and finely sliced

1 scallion, green part only, cut into long strips

sprigs of fresh cilantro, to garnish

1 Wash the rice in several changes of water until the water remains relatively clear. Drain well. Bring a large saucepan of salted water to a boil and add the rice. Cook for 12–15 minutes until tender. Drain well and set aside

2 Heat a wok, add the oil and, when very hot, add the garlic and stir-fry for 20 seconds or until just browned. Add the chilies and shrimp and stir-fry for 2–3 minutes.

3 Add the fish sauce, sugar, and soy sauce and stir-fry for another 30 seconds or until the shrimp are cooked through.

4 Add the cooked rice to the wok and stir together well. Then add the onion, red bell pepper, and scallion, mix together for an additional 1 minute, then turn onto a serving platter. Garnish with sprigs of fresh cilantro and serve immediately.

FOOD FACT

Thai fragrant, or jasmine rice is a good quality long-grain rice with a delicate scent, similar to basmati rice. The rice should be washed in several changes of water until the water remains relatively clear and then drained thoroughly. Cook the rice according to the directions on the package.

SPICED TOMATO PILAU

INGREDIENTS   Serves 2–3

1 cup basmati rice
¼ stick unsalted butter, plus
  1 tbsp.
4 green cardamom pods
2 star anise
4 whole cloves
10 black peppercorns
2 in. (5 cm) piece cinnamon
  stick

1 large red onion, peeled and
  finely sliced
6 oz. (175 g) can chopped
  tomatoes
salt and freshly ground black
  pepper
sprigs of fresh cilantro, to
  garnish

1 Wash the rice in several changes of water until the water remains relatively clear. Drain the rice and cover with fresh water. Let soak for 30 minutes. Drain well and set aside.

2 Heat the wok, then melt the butter and add the cardamoms, star anise, cloves, black peppercorns, and the cinnamon stick. Cook gently for 30 seconds. Increase the heat and add the onion. Stir-fry for 7–8 minutes until tender and starting to brown. Add the drained rice and cook an additional 2–3 minutes.

3 Strain the tomatoes and mix with sufficient warm water to make 2 cups. Pour this into the wok, season to taste with salt and pepper and bring to a boil.

4 Cover, reduce the heat to very low and cook for 10 minutes. Remove the wok from the heat and leave, covered for an additional 10 minutes. Do not lift the lid during cooking or resting. Finally, uncover and mix well with a fork, heat for 1 minute, then garnish with the sprigs of fresh cilantro and serve immediately.

HELPFUL HINT

The whole spices in this recipe are not meant to be eaten. Remove them before serving.

CHICKEN WITH NOODLES

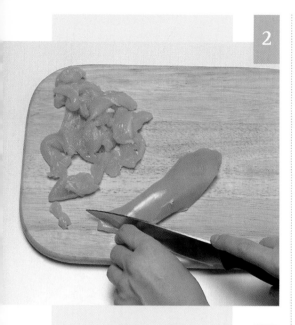

INGREDIENTS

Serves 2–3

3¼ cups medium egg noodles

¼ lb. (125 g) skinless, boneless chicken breast fillets

1 tbsp. light soy sauce

2 tsp. Chinese rice wine or dry sherry

5 tsp. peanut oil

2 garlic cloves, peeled and finely chopped

½ cup snow peas

2 tbsp. bacon, cut into fine strips

½ tsp. sugar

2 scallions, peeled and finely chopped

1 tsp. sesame oil

1 Cook the noodles according to the package directions. Drain and refresh under cold water. Drain again and set aside.

2 Slice the chicken into fine shreds and mix with 2 teaspoons of the light soy sauce and Chinese rice wine. Allow to marinate in the refrigerator for 10 minutes.

3 Heat a wok, add 2 teaspoons of the oil and, when hot, stir-fry the chicken shreds for about 2 minutes, then transfer to a plate. Wipe the wok clean with absorbent paper towels.

4 Return the wok to the heat and add the remaining oil. Add the garlic, then after 10 seconds add the snow peas and bacon. Stir-fry for an additional 1 minute, then add the drained noodles, remaining soy sauce, sugar, and scallions. Stir-fry for an additional 2 minutes, then add the reserved chicken.

5 Stir-fry for an additional 3–4 minutes until the chicken is cooked through. Add the sesame oil and mix together. Serve either hot or cold.

FOOD FACT

Chow mein literally means "stir-fried noodles." There are no hard and fast rules about which meat, fish or vegetables can be used. Chow mein also makes a tasty salad if served cold.

CHINESE BEAN SAUCE NOODLES

INGREDIENTS

Serves 4

3¾ cups fine egg noodles
1½ tbsp. sesame oil
1 tbsp. peanut oil
3 garlic cloves, peeled and
  finely chopped
4 scallions, trimmed and finely
  chopped
2 cups fresh ground pork
½ cup crushed yellow bean
  sauce
1-2 tsp. hot chili sauce

1 tbsp. Chinese rice wine or
  dry sherry
2 tbsp. dark soy sauce
½ tsp. cayenne pepper
2 tsp. sugar
⅔ cup chicken stock

1 Put the noodles into a large bowl and pour over boiling water to cover. Let soak according to the package directions until tender. Drain well and place in a bowl with the sesame oil. Toss together well and set aside.

2 Heat a wok until it is hot, add the peanut oil and, when hot, add the garlic and half the scallions. Stir-fry for a few seconds, then add the pork. Stir well to break up and continue to stir-fry for 1–2 minutes until it changes color.

3 Add the yellow bean sauce, chili sauce, Chinese rice wine or sherry, soy sauce, cayenne pepper, sugar, and chicken stock, stirring all the time. Bring to a boil, reduce the heat and simmer for 5 minutes.

4 Meanwhile bring a large saucepan of water to a boil and add the noodles for about 20 seconds. Drain well and tip into a warmed serving bowl. Pour the sauce over the top, sprinkle with the remaining scallions and mix well. Serve immediately.

FOOD FACT

Yellow bean sauce is a thick, spicy sauce made with yellow beans, flour, and salt fermented together. It is quite salty but adds a distinctive flavor. Available as whole beans in a thick sauce or as mashed beans (also known as crushed bean sauce). The whole bean sauce tends to be less salty.

Beef Noodle Soup

INGREDIENTS   Serves 4

2 lb. (900 g) boneless shin or
  braising steak
1 cinnamon stick
2 star anise
2 tbsp. light soy sauce
6 dried red chilies or 3 fresh,
  chopped in half
2 dried candied citrus
  peels, soaked and
  diced (optional)
5 cups beef or chicken stock

4¾ cups egg noodles
2 scallions, trimmed and
  chopped, to garnish
warm chunks of crusty
  farmhouse bread, to
  serve (optional)

1 Trim the meat of any fat and sinew, then cut into thin strips. Place the meat, cinnamon, star anise, soy sauce, red chilies, chopped candied citrus peels (if using), and stock in the wok. Bring to a boil, then reduce the heat to a simmer. Skim any fat or scum that floats to the surface. Cover the wok and simmer for about 1½ hours or until the meat is tender.

2 Meanwhile bring a saucepan of lightly salted water to a boil, then add the noodles and cook in the boiling water for 3–4 minutes until tender or according to the package directions. Drain well and set aside.

3 When the meat is tender, add the noodles to the wok and simmer for an additional 1–2 minutes until the noodles are heated through thoroughly. Ladle the soup into warm shallow soup bowls or dishes and sprinkle with chopped scallions. Serve, if desired, with chunks of warm crusty bread.

HELPFUL HINT

It is important to use shin or braising steak for this recipe because of the long cooking time required. A leaner cut of meat will end up dry and chewy.

CHICKEN NOODLE SOUP

INGREDIENTS   Serves 4

carcass of a medium-sized
cooked chicken

1 large carrot, peeled and
coarsely chopped

1 medium onion, peeled and
quartered

1 leek, trimmed and coarsely
chopped

2–3 bay leaves

a few black peppercorns

6½ cups water

5 cups Chinese cabbage or
bok choy, trimmed

½ cup chestnut mushrooms,
wiped and sliced

1¼ cups cooked chicken, sliced
or chopped

1 cup medium or fine egg
thread noodles

1 Break the chicken carcass into smaller pieces and place in the wok with the carrot, onion, leek, bay leaves, peppercorns, and water. Bring slowly to a boil. Skim away any fat or scum that rises to the surface for the first 15 minutes. Simmer very gently for 1–1½ hours. If the liquid reduces by more than one third, add a little more water.

2 Remove from the heat and leave until cold. Strain into a large bowl and chill in the refrigerator until any fat in the stock rises and sets on the surface. Remove the fat and discard. Draw a sheet of absorbent paper towel across the surface of the stock to absorb any remaining fat.

3 Return the stock to the wok and bring to a simmer. Add the Chinese cabbage, mushrooms, and chicken and simmer gently for 7–8 minutes until the vegetables are tender.

4 Meanwhile cook the noodles according to the package directions until tender. Drain well. Transfer a portion of noodles to each serving bowl before pouring in some soup and vegetables. Serve immediately.

HELPFUL HINT

This is an excellent way to
use up any leftover chicken as
well as the carcass from
a roast chicken.

CRISPY NOODLE SALAD

INGREDIENTS   Serves 4

2 tbsp. sunflower seeds
2 tbsp. pumpkin seeds
1 cup rice vermicelli or
  stir-fry noodles
1½ sticks unsalted butter
2 tbsp. sesame seeds,
  lightly toasted
1 cup red cabbage, trimmed
  and shredded
1 orange bell pepper, seeded
  and finely chopped

1 cup button mushrooms,
  wiped and quartered
2 scallions, trimmed and finely
  chopped
salt and freshly ground black
  pepper
shredded pickled sushi ginger,
  to garnish

1 Preheat the oven to 400° F (200° C), then sprinkle the sunflower and pumpkin seeds on a baking tray. Toast in the oven, stirring occasionally for 10–15 minutes or until lightly toasted. Remove from the oven and let cool.

2 Crush the rice vermicelli into small pieces (this is easiest while the noodles are still in the package), and set aside. Melt the butter in a small saucepan and let cool for a few minutes. Pour the clear yellow liquid carefully into a bowl, leaving behind the white milky solids. Discard the milky solids.

3 Heat the yellow, clarified butter in a wok and fry the crushed noodles in batches until browned, stirring constantly and gently. Remove the fried noodles as they cook, using a slotted spoon, and drain on absorbent

paper towels. Transfer the noodles to a bowl and add the toasted seeds.

4 Mix together the red cabbage, orange bell pepper, button mushrooms, and scallions in a large bowl and season to taste with salt and pepper. Just before serving, add the noodles and seeds to the salad and mix gently. Garnish with a little sushi ginger and serve.

HELPFUL HINT

Do not leave the salad to stand after adding the crispy noodles, as the moisture in the vegetables will cause them to wilt and soften.

THAI SPICY SHRIMP & LETTUCE NOODLE SOUP

INGREDIENTS

Serves 4

½ lb. (225 g) raw jumbo shrimp
1 tbsp. peanut or vegetable oil
2 garlic cloves, peeled and crushed
1 red chili, seeded and finely chopped
1 tbsp. freshly shredded ginger
4 scallions, trimmed and finely sliced
5 cups chicken stock
1 kaffir lime leaf, finely shredded

1 lemon grass stalk, outer leaves discarded and finely chopped
¾ cup shiitake mushrooms, sliced
1⅔ cups medium egg thread noodles
¾ cup lettuce, shredded
1 cup beansprouts

1 Shell the shrimp, leaving the tail tip on. Cut almost in half down the back of the shrimp, discarding any dark veins and open out. Rinse lightly, then pat dry with absorbent paper towels and set aside.

2 Heat a wok until very hot, then add the oil and, when hot, add the garlic, chili, ginger, and scallions and stir-fry for 30 seconds. Add the shrimp and stir-fry for an additional 1 minute.

3 Add the chicken stock, lime leaf, and lemon grass and bring to a boil. Reduce the heat and simmer for 10 minutes, adding the mushrooms after 7–8 minutes.

4 Meanwhile cook the noodles in plenty of boiling water according to the package directions.

Drain well. Add to the soup with the lettuce and beansprouts and return to a boil; simmer for about 30 seconds. Divide the soup among individual soup bowls and serve immediately.

FOOD FACT

Kaffir lime leaves are an essential ingredient in Thai cooking and impart a pungent lemon-lime flavor. They are not to be confused with limes, which are grown in Europe, whose leaves are larger and paler in color. The skin of the kaffir lime itself imparts a similar flavor. Lime leaves are available in Asian grocery stores, usually sold in bags or on stalks and they freeze well.

SEAFOOD NOODLE SALAD

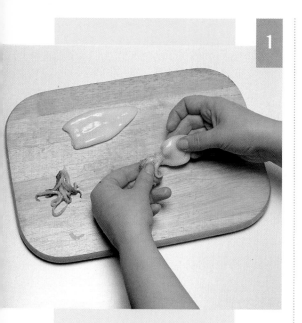

INGREDIENTS   Serves 4

8 baby squid, cleaned
2 tbsp. mirin
2 tbsp. rice vinegar
4 tbsp. corn oil
1 red chili, seeded and finely
  chopped
2 garlic cloves, peeled and
  crushed
6 scallions, trimmed
  and finely sliced

1 red bell pepper, seeded and
  finely sliced
1 tbsp. turmeric
2 tsp. ground coriander
8 raw jumbo shrimp, shelled
2½ cups medium egg noodles
¾ cup fresh white crabmeat
⅓ cup beansprouts
salt and freshly ground black
  pepper

1 Remove the tentacles from the squid and set aside. Slit the squid bodies open down one side and open out flat.

2 Using a small sharp knife, score the flesh diagonally, first in one direction then the other, to make diamond shapes. Place in a bowl with the squid tentacles, mirin, rice vinegar, half the oil, and the chili and marinate in the refrigerator for 1 hour.

3 Heat a wok until very hot. Add the remaining oil and, when hot, add the garlic, half the scallions, and the red bell pepper. Stir-fry for 1 minute, then add the turmeric and coriander. Cook for an additional 30 seconds before adding the cleaned squid and its marinade and the shrimp. Bring to a boil and simmer for 2–3 minutes or until the squid and shrimp are tender. Remove from the heat and let cool.

4 Cook the noodles for 3–4 minutes until tender or according to the package directions. Drain well and put in a large serving bowl with the crabmeat and the cooled squid and shrimp mixture. Stir together and leave until cold. Just before serving, add the beansprouts and remaining scallions with seasoning to taste and serve.

HELPFUL HINT

Supermarkets with fresh fish counters usually sell baby squid that is cleaned. If they are not available, buy a large squid weighing about ¾ lb. (350 g). Have the fish merchant clean it, then treat it in the same way as the baby squid described in step 1. Instead of scoring the flesh, cut it into 2 inch (5 cm) squares and cook as above.

CHINESE FRIED RICE

INGREDIENTS   Serves 4

2 cups long-grain rice
2 tbsp. peanut oil
¼ cup bacon, chopped
2 garlic cloves, peeled and
  finely chopped
1 tsp. freshly grated ginger
1 cup frozen peas, thawed
2 medium eggs, beaten
¾ cup beansprouts
salt and freshly ground black
  pepper

TO GARNISH:
½ cup roasted peanuts,
  chopped
3 scallions, trimmed and finely
  chopped

1 Wash the rice in several changes of water until it runs relatively clear. Drain well. Put into a saucepan or flameproof casserole dish with a tight-fitting lid. Pour in enough water to cover the rice by about ½ inch (1 cm). Add salt and bring to a boil. As soon as the water boils, cover the saucepan, reduce the heat as low as possible and cook for 10 minutes. Remove from the heat and let stand for an additional 10 minutes. Do not lift the lid while cooking. Leave until cold, then stir with a fork.

2 Heat a wok, add the oil and, when hot, add the bacon. Stir-fry for 1 minute before adding the garlic and ginger, then stir-fry for an additional 30 seconds.

3 Add the cooked rice and peas to the wok. Stir-fry over a high heat for 5 minutes.

4 Add the eggs and the beansprouts and continue to stir-fry for an additional 2 minutes until the eggs have set. Season to taste with salt and pepper. Spoon the mixture onto a serving plate and garnish with the peanuts and scallions. Serve hot or cold.

TASTY TIP

This dish is an excellent accompaniment to plain broiled chicken or fish or to serve with any meat that has been marinated with Chinese flavors.

HONEY-GLAZED DUCK IN KUMQUAT SAUCE

INGREDIENTS

Serves 4

4 duck breast fillets
1 tbsp. light soy sauce
1 tsp. sesame oil
1 tbsp. honey
3 tbsp. brandy
1 tbsp. corn oil
2 tbsp. sugar
1 tbsp. white wine vinegar
⅔ cup orange juice
1 cup kumquats, thinly sliced
2 tsp. cornstarch

salt and freshly ground black pepper
fresh watercress, to garnish
basmati and wild rice, to serve

1 Thinly slice the duck breasts and put in a shallow bowl. Mix together the soy sauce, sesame oil, honey, and 1 tablespoon of brandy. Pour over the duck, stir well, cover and marinate in the refrigerator for at least 1 hour.

2 Heat a wok until hot, add the corn oil and swirl it around to coat the sides. Drain the duck, setting aside the marinade, and stir-fry over a high heat until browned. Remove from the wok and set aside.

3 Wipe the wok clean with absorbent paper towels. Add the sugar, vinegar, and 1 tablespoon of water. Heat until the sugar dissolves, then boil until a rich golden color. Pour in the orange juice, then the remaining brandy. Stir in the kumquat slices and simmer for 5 minutes.

4 Blend the cornstarch with 1 tablespoon of cold water. Add to the wok and simmer for 2–3 minutes, stirring until thickened. Return the duck to the wok and cook gently for 1–2 minutes or until warmed through. Season to taste with salt and pepper. Spoon onto warmed plates and garnish with fresh watercress leaves. Serve immediately with freshly cooked basmati and wild rice.

FOOD FACT

Kumquats are tiny citrus fruits that resemble miniature oranges. They have a strong sharp/sweet flavor and are entirely edible, skin and all. They often contain many seeds, so it is worth halving or slicing them before using.

APPLE-TOSSED PORK

INGREDIENTS   Serves 4

¾ lb. (350 g) pork fillet
2 tbsp. all-purpose flour
salt and freshly ground black
    pepper
1½ tbsp. corn oil
1 tbsp. unsalted butter
2 eating apples, peeled, cored,
    and thinly sliced
2 tsp. mustard
1 tbsp. freshly chopped
    sage

2 tbsp. Calvados or apple
    brandy
4 tbsp. sour cream
fresh sage leaves, to garnish
freshly cooked green beans,
    to serve

1 Trim away any visible fat from the pork fillet, then cut across into ½ inch (1 cm) thick slices. Season the flour, then add the pork slices a few at a time and toss until lightly coated.

2 Heat a wok, then add the oil and heat. Stir-fry the meat in 2 batches over a fairly high heat until well browned. Remove from the wok and set aside.

3 Melt the butter slowly in the wok, add the apple slices and cook, stirring all the time for 1 minute. Stir in the mustard, chopped sage, Calvados brandy, and sour cream. Bring to a boil, stirring.

4 Return the pork and any juices to the wok and cook over a gentle heat for 1–2 minutes or until the meat has warmed through, the apples are just tender, and the sauce is

bubbling. Spoon onto warmed plates, garnish with fresh sage leaves and serve immediately with freshly cooked green beans.

TASTY TIP

For an easy braised red cabbage recipe to serve with the pork, thinly slice 1 onion and 3½ cups red cabbage. Heat 2 tablespoons vegetable or olive oil in a large saucepan and add the onion and cabbage along with 1 teaspoon of caraway seeds. Cook very gently, stirring occasionally for 10 minutes. Then add ⅔ cup vegetable or chicken stock, cover and simmer gently for about 1–1½ hours or until tender, adding a little extra stock or water if necessary.

MIXED APPETIZERS

INGREDIENTS   Serves 12

FOR THE STIR-FRIED CHEESE APPETIZERS:
6 thick slices white bread
½ stick butter, softened, plus 1 tbsp.
¾ cup mature cheddar cheese, shredded
¾ cup blue cheese such as Gorgonzola, crumbled
3 tbsp. corn oil

FOR THE SPICY NUTS:
¼ stick unsalted butter
2 tbsp. light olive oil
4 cups mixed unsalted nuts
1 tsp. ground paprika
½ tsp. ground cumin
½ tsp. fine sea salt
sprigs of fresh cilantro, to garnish

1 For the cheese appetizers, cut the crusts off the bread, then gently roll with a rolling pin to flatten slightly. Thinly spread with butter, then sprinkle over the mixed cheeses as evenly as possible.

2 Roll up each slice tightly, then cut into 4 slices, each about 1 inch (2.5 cm) long. Heat the oil in a wok or large skillet and stir-fry the cheese rolls in 2 batches, turning them all the time until golden brown and crisp. Drain on absorbent paper towels and serve warm or cold.

3 For the spicy nuts, melt the butter and oil in a wok, then add the nuts and stir-fry over a low heat for about 5 minutes, stirring all the time or until they begin to color.

4 Sprinkle the paprika and cumin over the nuts and continue stir-frying for an additional 1–2 minutes, or until the nuts are golden brown.

5 Remove from the wok and drain on absorbent paper towels. Sprinkle with the salt, garnish with sprigs of fresh cilantro and serve hot or cold. If serving cold, store both the cheese appetizers and the spicy nuts in airtight containers.

TASTY TIP

These appetizers are perfect for serving at a buffet or finger food party, or you can halve the quantities and serve with drinks instead of a starter at an informal dinner party for four to six people.

KUNG-PAO LAMB

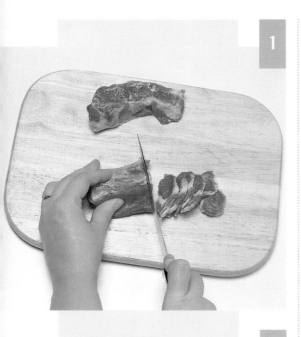

INGREDIENTS   Serves 4

1 lb. (450 g) lamb fillet
2 tbsp. soy sauce
2 tbsp. Chinese rice wine or
 dry sherry
2 tbsp. corn oil
2 tsp. sesame oil
½ cup unsalted peanuts
1 garlic clove, peeled and
 crushed
1 in. (2.5 cm) piece fresh
 ginger, finely chopped
1 red chili, seeded and finely
 chopped

1 small green bell pepper,
 seeded and diced
6 scallions, trimmed and
 diagonally sliced
½ cup lamb or vegetable stock
1 tsp. red wine vinegar
1 tsp. light brown sugar
2 tsp. cornstarch
plain boiled or steamed white
 rice, to serve

1 Wrap the lamb in parchment paper and place in the freezer for about 30 minutes until stiff. Cut the meat across the grain into paper thin slices. Put in a shallow bowl, add 2 teaspoons of the soy sauce and all the Chinese rice wine or sherry, and allow to marinate in the refrigerator for 15 minutes.

2 Heat a wok or skillet until hot, add the corn oil and swirl it around to coat the sides. Add the lamb and stir-fry for about 1 minute until lightly browned. Remove from the wok or skillet and set aside, leaving any juices behind.

3 Add the sesame oil to the wok or skillet and stir-fry the peanuts, garlic, ginger, chili, green bell pepper, and scallions for 1–2 minutes or until the nuts are golden. Return the lamb with the remaining soy sauce, stock, vinegar, and sugar.

4 Blend the cornstarch with 1 tablespoon of water. Stir in and cook the mixture for 1–2 minutes or until the vegetables are tender and the sauce has thickened. Serve immediately with plain boiled or steamed white rice.

FOOD FACT

No one knows exactly who Kung-Pao was; some believe he was an emperor, others a famous cook—only this famous and delicious stir-fry remains as a tribute.

SHRIMP SPECIAL FRIED RICE

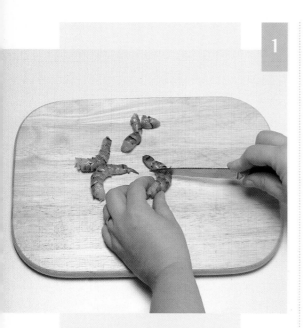

INGREDIENTS

Serves 4

2 cups raw shrimp, shelled
2 tbsp. light soy sauce
1 tsp. sugar
1 in. (2.5 cm) piece fresh
 ginger, peeled and grated
4 medium eggs
pinch of salt
1 tbsp. freshly chopped
 cilantro
2 tbsp. freshly chopped
 parsley

3 tbsp. corn oil
1 bunch scallions, trimmed
 and finely sliced
3¾ cups cooked long-grain rice
½ cup frozen peas, thawed
freshly ground black pepper

1 Using a small, sharp knife, remove the thin black thread that runs down the back of the shrimp, then rinse and pat dry with paper towels. Chop in half or thirds, then place in a bowl with the soy sauce, sugar, and ginger. Mix well and set aside.

2 Beat together 2 of the eggs with salt, the chopped cilantro, and parsley. Heat 1 tablespoon of the oil in a wok over a low heat and pour in the egg mixture. Tilt the wok so the mixture spreads to an even layer.

3 Cook gently, stirring until the mixture begins to set, then stop stirring and cook for an additional 30 seconds until the underneath is golden brown and the top is slightly creamy. Tip the omelet onto a clean chopping board and let cool. When cold, roll up loosely and cut into fine slices. Wipe the wok clean.

4 Heat the remaining oil and stir-fry the shrimp for 2–3 minutes or until they are cooked and have turned pink. Add the scallions and continue stir-frying for an additional 1–2 minutes.

5 Add the rice and peas and stir-fry for 2 minutes. Lightly beat the remaining 2 eggs. Drizzle over the rice, then stir-fry for about 30 seconds until scrambled. Serve immediately, sprinkled with the shredded omelet.

TASTY TIP

Using raw shrimp gives this dish a freshness that cooked shrimp would not. They have a much better texture and shrink far less than their cooked counterparts.

CREAMY CHICKEN STROGANOFF

INGREDIENTS

Serves 4

1 lb.(450 g) skinless chicken
  breast fillets
4 tbsp. dry sherry
2 tbsp. dried porcini
  mushrooms
2 tbsp. corn oil
¼ stick unsalted butter
1 onion, peeled and sliced
2 cups chestnut mushrooms,
  wiped and sliced
1 tbsp. paprika
1 tsp. freshly chopped thyme

½ cup chicken stock
⅔ cup sour cream
salt and freshly ground black
  pepper
sprigs of fresh thyme, to
  garnish

TO SERVE:
sour cream
freshly cooked rice or
  egg noodles

1 Cut the chicken into finger length strips and set aside. Gently warm the sherry in a small saucepan and remove from the heat. Add the porcini mushrooms and let soak while preparing the rest of the stir fry.

2 Heat a wok, add 1½ tablespoons of the oil and, when hot, add the chicken and stir-fry over a high heat for 3–4 minutes or until browned. Remove from the wok and set aside.

3 Heat the remaining oil and butter in the wok and cook the onion for 5 minutes. Add the chestnut mushrooms and stir-fry for an additional 5 minutes or until tender. Sprinkle in the paprika and thyme and cook for 30 seconds.

4 Add the porcini mushrooms with their soaking liquid,

then stir in the stock and return the chicken to the wok. Cook for 1–2 minutes or until the chicken is cooked through and tender.

5 Stir in the sour cream and heat until piping hot. Season to taste with salt and pepper. Garnish with sprigs of fresh thyme and serve immediately with a spoonful of sour cream and rice or egg noodles.

HELPFUL HINT

Dried porcini mushrooms should be soaked in very hot but not boiling water for at least 20 minutes. Use the soaking liquor as well as the rehydrated mushrooms in order to obtain maximum flavor from the mushrooms.

QUICK MEDITERRANEAN SHRIMP

INGREDIENTS

Serves 4

20 raw jumbo shrimp
3 tbsp. olive oil
1 garlic clove, peeled and
  crushed
2 tsp. finely grated lemon zest
1 tbsp. lemon juice
sprigs of fresh rosemary

FOR THE PESTO & SUNDRIED TOMATO DIPS:
⅔ cup plain yogurt
1 tbsp. prepared pesto
⅔ cup sour cream
1 tbsp. sundried tomato paste
1 tbsp. mustard
salt and freshly ground black
  pepper
lemon wedges, to garnish

1 Remove the shells from the shrimp, leaving the tail shells. Using a small, sharp knife, remove the dark vein that runs along the back of the shrimp. Rinse and drain on absorbent paper towels.

2 Beat 2 tablespoons of the oil with the garlic, lemon zest, and juice in a small bowl. Bruise 1 sprig of rosemary with a rolling pin and add to the bowl. Add the shrimp, toss to coat, then cover and allow to marinate in the refrigerator until needed.

3 For the simple dips, mix the yogurt and pesto in one bowl and the sour cream, tomato paste, and mustard in another bowl. Season to taste with salt and pepper.

4 Heat a wok, add the remaining oil and swirl around to coat the sides. Remove the shrimp from the marinade, leaving any juices and the rosemary behind. Add to the wok and stir-fry over a high heat for 3–4 minutes or until the shrimp are pink and just cooked through.

5 Remove the shrimp from the wok and arrange on a platter. Garnish with lemon wedges and more fresh rosemary sprigs and serve hot or cold with the dips.

HELPFUL HINT

The shrimp must be cooked thoroughly but take care not to overcook them or they will be tough. Remove from the refrigerator and leave at room temperature for 15 minutes before stir frying.

Sweet-&-Sour Shredded Beef

INGREDIENTS   Serves 4

¾ lb. (350 g) rump steak
1 tsp. sesame oil
2 tbsp. Chinese rice wine or
    sweet sherry
2 tbsp. dark soy sauce
1 tsp. cornstarch
4 tbsp. pineapple juice
2 tsp. light brown sugar
1 tsp. sherry vinegar
salt and freshly ground black
    pepper
2 tbsp. peanut oil

2 medium carrots, peeled and
    cut into matchsticks
1 cup snow peas, trimmed and
    cut into matchsticks
1 bunch scallions, trimmed
    and shredded
2 garlic cloves, peeled and
    crushed
1 tbsp. toasted sesame seeds
freshly cooked Thai fragrant
    rice, to serve

1 Cut the steak across the grain into thin strips. Put in a bowl with the sesame oil, 1 tablespoon of the Chinese rice wine or sherry, and 1 tablespoon of the soy sauce. Mix well, cover and allow to marinate in the refrigerator for 30 minutes.

2 In a small bowl, blend together the cornstarch with the remaining Chinese rice wine or sherry, then stir in the pineapple juice, remaining soy sauce, sugar, and vinegar. Season with a little salt and pepper and set aside.

3 Heat a wok until hot, add 1 tablespoon of the oil, then drain the beef, setting aside the marinade, and stir-fry for 1–2 minutes or until browned. Remove from the wok and set aside.

4 Add the remaining oil to the wok, then add the carrots and stir-fry for 1 minute, then add the snow peas and scallions and stir-fry for an additional 1 minute.

5 Return the beef to the wok with the sauce, reserved marinade, and garlic. Continue cooking for 1 minute or until the vegetables are tender and the sauce is bubbling. Turn the stir fry into a warmed serving dish, sprinkle with toasted sesame seeds and serve immediately with the Thai fragrant rice.

HELPFUL HINT

It is important to slice the beef across the grain so that it will hold together when it is being cooked.

VEGETABLE KOFTA CURRY

INGREDIENTS

Serves 6

3 cups potatoes, peeled and diced

1 cup carrots, peeled and coarsely chopped

1 cup parsnips, peeled and coarsely chopped

1 medium egg, lightly beaten

¾ cup all-purpose flour, sifted

⅓ cup corn oil

2 onions, peeled and sliced

2 garlic cloves, peeled and crushed

1 in. (2.5 cm) piece fresh ginger, peeled and shredded

2 tbsp. garam masala

2 tbsp. tomato paste

1¼ cups vegetable stock

1 cup plain yogurt

3 tbsp. freshly chopped cilantro

salt and freshly ground black pepper

1 Bring a saucepan of lightly salted water to a boil. Add the potatoes, carrots, and parsnips. Cover and simmer for 12–15 minutes or until the vegetables are tender. Drain the vegetables and mash until very smooth. Stir the egg into the vegetable purée, then add the flour and mix to make a stiff paste and set aside.

2 Heat 2 tablespoons of the oil in a wok and gently cook the onions for 10 minutes. Add the garlic and ginger and cook for an additional 2–3 minutes or until soft and just beginning to color.

3 Sprinkle the garam masala over the onions and stir in. Add the tomato paste and stock. Bring to a boil, cover and simmer gently for 15 minutes.

4 Meanwhile heat the remaining oil in a wok or skillet. Drop in tablespoons of vegetable batter, 4 or 5 at a time and fry, turning often for 3-4 minutes until brown and crisp. Remove with a slotted spoon and drain on absorbent paper towels. Keep warm in a low oven while cooking the rest.

5 Stir the yogurt and cilantro into the onion sauce. Slowly heat to boiling point and season to taste with salt and pepper. Divide the koftas among warmed serving plates and spoon over the sauce. Serve immediately.

FOOD FACT

Why not serve this dish with a plain or flavoured naan bread to mop up the delicious sauce.

BRANDIED BEEF

INGREDIENTS

Serves 4

1 lb. (450 g) rump steak
2 tsp. dark soy sauce
1 tsp. dark brown sugar
salt and freshly ground black
  pepper
1 small fennel bulb
1 red bell pepper
1 orange
2 tbsp. corn oil
1 tbsp. unsalted butter

2 cups tiny whole button
  mushrooms
5 tbsp. beef stock
3 tbsp. brandy
orange wedges, to garnish
freshly cooked rice or noodles,
  to serve

1 Trim any fat from the steak and cut across the grain into thin strips. Place in a shallow bowl with the soy sauce, sugar, and a little salt, and pepper. Mix well and allow to marinate while preparing the vegetables.

2 Trim the fennel and slice as thinly as possible, from the stems down through the root. Quarter, seed, and thinly slice the red bell pepper. Thinly pare the rind from about half the orange and cut into fine matchsticks. Squeeze out the juice.

3 Heat the oil and butter in a wok, add the beef and stir-fry for 2 minutes until brown and tender. Remove with a slotted spoon and set aside.

4 Add the fennel, red bell pepper, and mushrooms to the wok and stir-fry for 3–4 minutes or until softened. Add the orange zest, juice, and the stock and cook for 2 minutes until the sauce is reduced slightly. Return the beef to the wok and stir-fry for 30 seconds to heat through.

5 Heat the brandy in a small saucepan or ladel, ignite, then let the flames subside and pour over the vegetables and meat. Gently shake the wok occasionally until the flames subside. Garnish with a few orange wedges and serve immediately with rice or noodles.

HELPFUL HINT

If you prefer not to flame the brandy in the wok, simply simmer gently for about 5 minutes until the alcohol has evaporated, by which time it will have imparted its flavor to the food.

GARLIC MUSHROOMS WITH CRISPY BACON & CHICKEN LIVER SAUTÉ

INGREDIENTS   Serves 4

4 large field mushrooms
¼ stick butter, melted and
  cooled, plus 1 tbsp.
2 garlic cloves, peeled and
  crushed
1 tbsp. corn oil
3 slices bacon, derinded and
  chopped
4 shallots, peeled and thinly
  sliced

1 lb. (450 g) chicken livers,
  halved
2 tbsp. marsala or sweet
  sherry
4 tbsp. chicken or vegetable
  stock
6 tbsp. heavy cream
2 tsp. freshly chopped thyme
salt and freshly ground black
  pepper

1 Remove the stalks from the mushrooms and coarsely chop. Mix together ¼ stick of the butter and garlic and brush over both sides of the mushroom caps. Place on the rack of a broiler pan.

2 Heat a wok, add the oil and, when hot, add the bacon and stir-fry for 2–3 minutes or until crispy. Remove and set aside. Add the remaining butter to the wok and stir-fry the shallots and chopped mushroom stalks for 4–5 minutes until they are softened.

3 Add the chicken livers and cook for 3–4 minutes or until well browned on the outside but still pink and tender inside. Pour in the marsala or sherry and the stock. Simmer for 1 minute, then stir in the cream, thyme, salt, pepper, and half the

bacon. Cook for about 30 seconds to heat through.

4 While the livers are frying, cook the mushroom caps under a hot broiler for 3–4 minutes each side until tender.

5 Place the mushrooms on warmed serving plates, allowing one per person. Spoon the chicken livers over and around the mushrooms. Sprinkle with the remaining bacon and serve immediately.

FOOD FACT

This dish makes a wonderful starter for a dinner party or can be served with plain boiled or steamed rice and a green vegetable for an informal supper.

CHICKEN WRAPS

INGREDIENTS   Serves 4

FOR THE STIR-FRIED CHICKEN:
4 skinless chicken breast fillets
2 tsp. finely grated lime zest
1 tbsp. lime juice
1 tbsp. sugar
2 tsp. dried oregano
½ tsp. ground cinnamon
¼ tsp. cayenne pepper
3 tbsp. corn oil
2 onions, peeled and sliced
1 green, 1 red, and 1 yellow
  bell pepper, seeded and sliced

salt and freshly ground black
  pepper

FOR THE TORTILLAS:
2¼ cups all-purpose flour
pinch of salt
¼ tsp. baking powder
¼ cup white vegetable fat

TO SERVE:
sour cream
guacamole

1 Slice the chicken across the grain into ¾ inch (2 cm) wide strips. Place in a bowl with the lime zest, lime juice, sugar, oregano, cinnamon, and cayenne pepper. Mix well and marinate while making the tortillas.

2 Sift the flour, salt, and baking powder into a bowl. Rub in the white fat, then sprinkle over 4 tablespoons of warm water and mix to a stiff dough. Knead on a lightly floured surface for 10 minutes until smooth and elastic.

3 Divide the dough into 12 equal pieces and roll out each to a 6 inch (15 cm) circle. Cover with plastic wrap to prevent them drying out before you cook them.

4 Heat a nonstick wok and cook each tortilla for about 1 minute on each side or until golden and slightly blistered. Remove the tortillas and keep warm and pliable in a dish towel.

5 Heat 2 tablespoons of the oil in the wok and stir-fry the onions for 5 minutes until lightly colored. Remove with a slotted spoon and set aside.

6 Add the remaining oil to the wok and heat. Drain the chicken from the marinade and add it to the wok. Stir-fry for 5 minutes, then return the onions, add the bell pepper slices and cook for an additional 3–4 minutes or until the chicken is cooked through and the vegetables are tender. Season to taste with salt and pepper and serve immediately with the tortillas, sour cream, and guacamole.

SESAME-COATED TURKEY WITH MANGO TABBOULEH

INGREDIENTS   Serves 4

3 turkey breast fillets, skinned
4 tbsp. all-purpose flour
4 tbsp. sesame seeds
salt and freshly ground black
  pepper
1 medium egg, lightly beaten
2 tbsp. corn oil

**FOR THE MANGO
  TABBOULEH:**
1 cup bulgar
2 tbsp. olive oil
2 tbsp. lemon juice
6 scallions, trimmed and finely
  chopped
1 red chili, seeded and finely
  chopped
1 ripe mango, peeled, pitted,
  and diced
3 tbsp. freshly chopped
  cilantro
1 tbsp. freshly chopped mint
  leaves

1 Cut the turkey across the grain into strips. Mix together the flour, sesame seeds, salt, and pepper. Dip the turkey strips in the beaten egg, then in the sesame seed mixture to coat. Chill in the refrigerator until ready to cook.

2 For the tabbouleh, put the bulgar in a large bowl and pour over plenty of boiling water. Cover the bowl with a plate and let soak for 20 minutes.

3 Beat together the olive oil and lemon juice in a large bowl. Stir in the scallions, chili, mango, cilantro, and mint. Drain the bulgar and squeeze out any excess moisture with your hands, then add to the bowl, season to taste with salt and pepper and mix well.

4 Heat a wok, add the oil and, when hot, stir-fry the sesame-coated turkey strips in 2 batches for 4–5 minutes or until golden, crispy, and cooked through. Divide the turkey strips among individual serving plates and serve immediately with the tabbouleh.

FOOD FACT

Bulgar, sometimes called cracked wheat, is a common ingredient in Middle Eastern cookery. It has a nutty flavor and a firm texture and is equally delicious hot or cold.

SALMON TERIYAKI WITH NOODLES & CRISPY GREENS

INGREDIENTS   Serves 4

¾ lb. (350 g) salmon fillet
3 tbsp. Japanese soy sauce
3 tbsp. mirin or sweet sherry
3 tbsp. sake
1 tbsp. freshly shredded ginger
1½ cups spring greens
peanut oil for deep frying
pinch of salt
½ tsp. sugar
1⅔ cups cellophane noodles

TO GARNISH:
1 tbsp. freshly chopped dill
sprigs of fresh dill
2 tsp. lemon zest

1 Cut the salmon into paper thin slices and place in a shallow dish. Mix together the soy sauce, mirin or sherry, sake, and the ginger. Pour over the salmon, cover and allow to marinate for 15–30 minutes.

2 Remove and discard the thick stalks from the spring greens. Lay several leaves on top of each other, roll up tightly, then shred finely.

3 Pour in enough oil to cover about 2 inches (5 cm) of the wok. Deep-fry the greens in batches for about 1 minute each until crisp. Remove and drain on absorbent paper towels. Transfer to a serving dish, sprinkle with salt and sugar and toss together.

4 Place the noodles in a bowl and pour over warm water to cover. Let soak for 15–20 minutes until soft, then drain. With scissors cut into 6 inch (15 cm) lengths.

5 Preheat the broiler. Remove the salmon slices from the marinade, setting aside the marinade for later, and arrange them in a single layer on a baking tray. Broil for about 2 minutes until lightly cooked, without turning.

6 When the oil in the wok is cool enough, tip most of it away, leaving about 1 tablespoon behind. Heat until hot, then add the noodles and the reserved marinade and stir-fry for 3–4 minutes. Tip the noodles into a large serving bowl and arrange the salmon on top, garnished with chopped dill, sprigs of fresh dill, and lemon zest. Sprinkle with a little of the crispy greens and serve the rest separately.

CHICKEN TIKKA MASALA

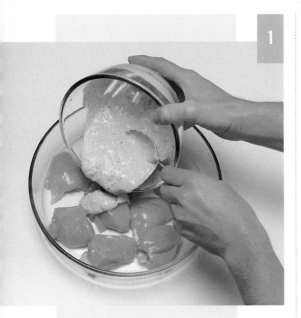

INGREDIENTS
Serves 4

4 skinless chicken breast fillets
⅔ cup plain yogurt
1 garlic clove, peeled and
  crushed
1 in. (2.5 cm) piece fresh
  ginger, peeled and shredded
1 tsp. chili powder
1 tbsp. ground coriander
2 tbsp. lime juice
twist of lime, to garnish
freshly cooked rice, to serve

FOR THE MASALA SAUCE:
1 tbsp. unsalted butter
2 tbsp. corn oil
1 onion, peeled and chopped
1 green chili, seeded and
  finely chopped
1 tsp. garam masala
½ cup heavy cream
salt and freshly ground black
  pepper
3 tbsp. fresh cilantro leaves,
  coarsely torn

1 Preheat the oven to 400° F (200° C), 15 minutes before cooking. Cut each chicken breast across into 3 pieces, then make 2 or 3 shallow cuts in each piece. Put in a shallow dish. Mix together the yogurt, garlic, ginger, chili powder, ground coriander, and lime juice. Pour over the chicken, cover and marinate in the refrigerator for up to 24 hours.

2 Remove the chicken from the marinade and arrange on a greased baking tray. Bake in the preheated oven for 15 minutes or until golden and cooked.

3 While the chicken is cooking, heat the butter and oil in a wok and stir-fry the onion for 5 minutes or until tender. Add the chili and garam masala and stir-fry for a few more seconds. Stir in the cream and remaining marinade. Simmer over a low heat for 1 minute, stirring all the time.

4 Add the chicken pieces and cook for an additional 1 minute, stirring to coat in the sauce. Season to taste with salt and pepper. Transfer the chicken pieces to a serving plate. Stir the chopped cilantro into the sauce, then spoon over the chicken, garnish and serve immediately with freshly cooked rice.

TASTY TIP

Make your own garam masala by grinding together ½ teaspoon cardamom seeds, 1 inch (2.5 cm) cinnamon stick, ½ teaspoon cumin seeds, ½ teaspoon cloves, ½ teaspoon black peppercorns, and 5 gratings of nutmeg, until fine.

MAPLE PEARS WITH PISTACHIOS & SIMPLE CHOCOLATE SAUCE

INGREDIENTS — Serves 4

¼ stick unsalted butter
½ cup unsalted pistachios
4 medium-ripe firm pears, peeled, quartered, and cored
2 tsp. lemon juice
pinch of ground ginger (optional)
6 tbsp. maple syrup

FOR THE CHOCOLATE SAUCE:
½ cup heavy cream
2 tbsp. milk
½ tsp. vanilla extract
5 squares unsweetened chocolate, broken into pieces and coarsely chopped

1 Melt the butter in a wok over a medium heat until sizzling. Turn down the heat a little, add the pistachios and stir-fry for 30 seconds.

2 Add the pears to the wok and continue cooking for about 2 minutes, turning frequently and carefully until the nuts are beginning to brown and the pears are tender.

3 Add the lemon juice, ground ginger if using, and maple syrup. Cook for 3–4 minutes or until the syrup has reduced slightly. Spoon the pears and the syrup into a serving dish and let cool for 1–2 minutes while making the chocolate sauce.

4 Pour the cream and milk into the wok. Add the vanilla extract and heat just to boiling point. Remove the wok from the heat.

5 Add the chocolate to the wok and leave for 1 minute to melt, then stir until the chocolate is evenly mixed with the cream. Pour into a jug and serve while still warm, with the pears.

FOOD FACT

Maple syrup is made by tapping maple trees in early spring when the sap is running. The thin clear liquid is boiled until brown and syrupy. Most commerical syrups are uniform in flavor and color but it is possible to find syrups made at later stages in the spring, with a richer character.

TIPSY TROPICAL FRUIT

INGREDIENTS   Serves 4

8 oz. (225 g) can pineapple
  chunks in natural juice
2 guavas
1 papaya
2 passion fruit
¼ stick unsalted butter
1 tbsp. orange juice
¼ cup creamed coconut,
  chopped
¼ cup firmly packed light
  brown sugar

2 tbsp. white rum
sprigs of fresh mint, to
  decorate
vanilla ice cream, to serve

1 Drain the pineapple chunks, setting aside the juice. Pat the pineapple dry on absorbent paper towels. Peel the guavas and cut into wedges. Halve the papaya and scoop out the black seeds. Peel and cut into 1 inch (2.5 cm) chunks. Halve the passion fruit and scoop out the seeds into a small bowl.

2 Heat the butter in a wok, add the pineapple and stir-fry over a high heat for 30 seconds. Turn down the heat and add the guavas and papaya. Drizzle over the orange juice and cook for 2 minutes, stirring occasionally, taking care not to break up the fruit.

3 Using a slotted spoon, remove the fruit from the wok, leaving any juices behind and transfer to a warmed serving dish. Add the creamed coconut to the wok with the sugar and pineapple juice. Simmer for 2–3 minutes, stirring until the coconut has melted.

4 Add the white rum to the wok and heat through, then pour over the fruit. Spoon the passion fruit pulp on top and serve hot with spoonfuls of ice cream decorated with a sprig of mint.

FOOD FACT

Passion fruit are small, round, purplish fruits, which are ripe when the skin is dimpled and wrinkled. To use them, it is necessary to slice them across the center and scoop out the seeds and flesh. The seeds are edible and have a lot of flavor but can be strained out if preferred.

FRUITED FRENCH TOAST

INGREDIENTS

Serves 4

8 slices spicy fruit loaf, about ½ in. (1 cm) thick
1 cup milk
3 tbsp. orange liqueur
2 medium egg yolks
¼ tsp. ground cinnamon
½ stick unsalted butter
1 tbsp. corn oil
5 tbsp. seedless raspberry jelly

FOR THE ORANGE-SCENTED CREAM:
½ cup heavy cream
1 tsp. confectioners' sugar
3 tsp. finely grated orange zest
1 tbsp. orange flower water

1 Cut the crusts off the bread, then cut each slice diagonally into 4 triangles. Mix together half the milk and 2 tablespoons of the liqueur. Quickly dip the bread triangles in the mixture, then place on a wire rack over a tray to drain.

2 Beat together the egg yolks, cinnamon, remaining milk, and any liqueur-flavored milk on the tray. Dip the triangles in the egg and return to the rack.

3 Heat half the butter and the oil in a wok. Add the bread triangles about 3 at a time and fry on both sides until well browned. Remove and keep warm in a low oven, while cooking the rest.

4 When needed, add the remaining butter and finish cooking the bread triangles. Add to those keeping warm in the oven while making the sauce.

5 Gently heat the jelly in the wok with the remaining 1 tablespoon of liqueur and 1 tablespoon of water until melted, then cook for 1 minute.

6 To make the orange-scented cream, whip the cream, confectioners' sugar, orange zest, and orange flower water together until soft peaks form. Serve the French toasts drizzled with the jelly sauce and accompanied by the orange-scented cream.

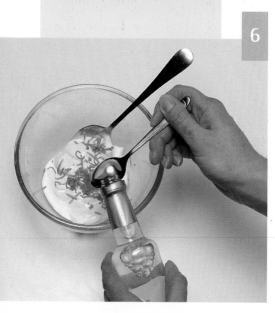

HELPFUL HINT

The hot butter needs to be watched carefully in between batches. It may go brown, which will add a pleasant nutty flavor but it is important to make sure that it does not burn.

HOT CHERRY FRITTERS

INGREDIENTS   Serves 6

½ stick butter

pinch of salt

2 tbsp. sugar

1 cup all-purpose flour, sifted

¼ tsp. ground cinnamon

¼ cup ground almonds

3 medium eggs, lightly beaten

1 cup cherries, pitted

corn oil for frying

2 tbsp. confectioners' sugar

1 tsp. unsweetened cocoa

sprigs of fresh mint, to decorate

1 Place the butter, salt, and sugar in a small saucepan with 1 cup of water. Heat gently until the butter has melted, then add the flour and ground cinnamon and beat over a low heat until the mixture leaves the sides of the saucepan.

2 Remove the saucepan from the heat and beat in the ground almonds. Gradually add the eggs, beating well after each addition. Finally stir in the cherries.

3 Pour 2 inches (5 cm) depth of oil in a wok and heat until it reaches 350°F (180° C) on a sugar thermometer. Drop in heaped teaspoons of the mixture, cooking 4 or 5 at a time for about 2 minutes or until lightly browned and crisp.

4 Remove the fritters from the wok with a slotted spoon and drain on absorbent paper towels. Keep warm in a low oven while cooking the remaining fritters. Arrange on a warmed serving plate and dust with the confectioners' sugar and unsweetened cocoa. Decorate with mint sprigs and serve hot.

HELPFUL HINT

It is essential to bring the oil back up to temperature each time before cooking the next batch of fritters.

STIR-FRIED BANANAS & PEACHES WITH RUM BUTTERSCOTCH SAUCE

INGREDIENTS   Serves 4

2 medium-firm bananas
1 tbsp. sugar
2 tsp. lime juice
4 firm, ripe peaches or
   nectarines
1 tbsp. corn oil

**FOR THE RUM
BUTTERSCOTCH SAUCE:**
½ stick unsalted butter
¼ cup firmly packed light
   brown sugar
½ cup raw sugar
½ cup heavy cream
2 tbsp. dark rum

1 Peel the bananas and cut into 1 inch (2.5 cm) diagonal slices. Place in a bowl and sprinkle with the sugar and lime juice and stir until lightly coated. Set aside.

2 Place the peaches or nectarines in a large bowl and pour over boiling water to cover. Leave for 30 seconds, then plunge them into cold water and peel off their skins. Cut each one into 8 thick slices, discarding the pit.

3 Heat a wok, add the oil and swirl it around the wok to coat the sides. Add the fruit and cook for 3–4 minutes, shaking the wok and gently turning the fruit until lightly browned. Spoon the fruit into a warmed serving bowl and clean the wok with absorbent paper towels.

4 Add the butter and sugars to the wok and stir continuously over a very low heat until the sugar has dissolved. Remove from the heat and let cool for 2–3 minutes.

5 Stir the cream and rum into the sugar syrup and return to the heat. Bring to a boil and simmer for 2 minutes, stirring continuously until smooth. Leave for 2–3 minutes to cool slightly, then serve warm with the stir-fried peaches and bananas.

HELPFUL HINT

Bananas should not be prepared too far ahead of cooking as they tend to discolor. If necessary, dip them in a little lemon juice to stop them turning brown.

INDEX